Berlitz

Scotland

Front cover and left: aspects
of Eilean Donan Castle

TOP 10 ATTRACTIONS

Edinburgh The capital has everything: a castle, a palace, a parliament, an international arts festival, haute cuisine... *(page 27)*

Glen Coe • Its stunning scenery is a magnet for hikers *(page 74)*

Culzean Castle
Spectacularly positioned on a cliff's edge, it dates from the 16th century *(page 47)*

Burrell Collection
Glasgow's treasure trove of outstanding art *(page 51)*

Loch Lomond Britain's largest freshwater lake has fired the imagination of many a composer and writer, including Sir Walter Scott *(page 57)*

Skye The atmospheric isle has a number of dramatic rock formations *(page 81)*

Burns Country The Burns Trail runs from Alloway to Dumfries *(page 44)*

Urquhart Castle A romantic ruin by Loch Ness that may have been the site of a Pictish fort *(page 70)*

Inverewe Garden Overlooking Loch Ewe, here subtropical flora and fauna thrive *(page 75)*

St Andrews On the Fife coast is the home of golf and Scotland's oldest university *(page 59)*

A PERFECT DAY

8.30am Breakfast

The ideal place to start a day of culture is at the Scottish Café inside the National Gallery of Scotland, on Princes Street. Set yourself up with a traditional breakfast before a look around the gallery.

10.00am Edinburgh Castle

Follow the Mound, crossing Princes Street Gardens towards the Old Town and climb the steep steps up to the castle. It's worth getting to the castle early to avoid the crowds. From here there are great views across the New Town below.

11.30am Castle Hill

Walk back down Castle Hill, passing attractions such as the Scotch Whisky Experience, Camera Obscura and Gladstone's Land, along the way. Take time to explore the vennels and wynds as you go.

12.30pm Shopping

Off George V Bridge, visit Victoria Street with its specialist shops, and continue on into the Grassmarket for lots of lunch options. Retrace your steps and continue to High Street, where St Giles Cathedral dominates.

IN EDINBURGH

3.00pm Holyroodhouse

It is worth taking time to see the fine collection of royal artefacts (if the royal family are not in residence); alternatively, if weather allows, explore the huge expanse of Holyrood Park behind.

2.00pm Royal Mile

Continue down the Royal Mile, where you will find notable attractions including the Museum of Childhood, John Knox House, the Museum of Edinburgh and Canongate Tolbooth. Near the end of the road, the Scottish Parliament Building looms into view and at the foot of the Royal Mile stands the Palace of Holyroodhouse.

4.00pm Afternoon tea

Walk back up the Royal Mile. Just past the Scottish Parliament building is Clarinda's Tearoom, a great pit stop to indulge in tea and home-baked treats.

7.30pm Dinner

After freshening up at your hotel, head to the New Town – in and around George Street, good places to eat are endless. If Mediterranean cooking is your preference, try the ever-popular Gusto or Librizzi's. For a special occasion, Oloroso offers stunning views.

9.30pm On the town

You couldn't be in a better spot to finish the night in a chic bar or nightclub. On George Street, pop into the Opal Lounge for cocktails and then move onto Lulu, a trendy club housed in the Tigerlilly hotel; or perhaps Bacaro in nearby Hope Street for heaps of sophistication.

CONTENTS

37

90

79

98

60

84

INTRODUCTION

Scotland is a land steeped in romantic tradition. Its distinctive dress, its national drink, its famous bagpipe music and its stormy history give it an image recognisable worldwide. Though Scotland's territory is small, it has an unrivalled variety of landscape: deep green glens that slice through rugged mountains; forbidding castles reflected in dark, peat-stained lochs; moors awash with purple heather or yellow broom and gorse; green fields and hills dotted with sheep; and a wildly irregular coastline, incessantly pounded by the Atlantic and the North Sea, with both forbidding cliffs and sweeping sandy beaches.

Scotland's Highlands and Islands are a riot of spectacular natural beauty and one of the few remaining wilderness frontiers in all of Europe. Within easy reach of the cities of Edinburgh, Glasgow and Aberdeen are vast tracts of unspoiled country. You might see red deer break cover and golden eagles, or even an osprey, swooping overhead. In coursing streams, magnificent salmon and trout challenge the angler, while seals lounge on rocky shores. It's quite possible to walk all day and not see another human being.

The sea flows in to fill many of the country's 300 lochs (except for the Lake of Menteith, Scots never call them 'lakes'); others are fresh water. The rolling hills and tranquil rivers of the south and the rich farmland of Fife and Royal Deeside present gentler but no less enticing landscapes.

The cultural mosaic, like the scenery, is hugely varied. Every summer Edinburgh, the intellectually and architecturally stimulating capital, is the scene of a distinguished international festival of music and the arts; and Glasgow is

Stags in the Scottish Highlands

Glasgow's School of Art

a former 'European City of Culture'. Both cities have outstanding museums and the Burrell Collection in Glasgow is one of Europe's great art galleries. All around the country you'll find theatre festivals, concerts, Highland gatherings, folk shows and crafts exhibitions. You can visit some 150 castles – some intact, others respectable ruins. There are also baronial mansions, ancient abbeys and archaeological sites that invite exploration. The Gulf Stream along the west coast makes it possible for subtropical gardens to flourish.

Geography and Climate

Covering the northernmost third of the United Kingdom, Scotland's 77,700 sq miles (30,000 sq km) are home to more than 5 million Scots, making up one-tenth of the total population of Great Britain. Scotland's territorial area includes 790 islands, of which 130 are inhabited. Some are popular tourist destinations easily reached by ferry or plane.

Happily, what people say about Scotland's weather isn't always true. Between May and October there are hours and even whole days of hot sunshine interrupting the rain, mist and bracing winds which perhaps keep the Scots so hardy. Interestingly enough, Scotland in an average year enjoys as much sun as London. Sightseers and photographers appreciate the amazing visibility to be had on clear days. Around lochs and on the coast the only drawback is the midge. These pesky biting flies are impossible to avoid at the beginning and end of the day during the summer. The cold, snowy winters have made the Highlands Britain's skiing centre; there are many suitable areas for both downhill and cross-country skiing with Glen Coe having the steepest runs.

Politics and Identity

Constitutionally linked to England for nearly three centuries, Scotland is a land that keeps proudly unto itself. It prints its own bank notes (British versions circulate as well), and maintains independent educational and judicial systems, its own church, and more recently, its own Parliament. Gaelic is still spoken in the Western Highlands and Islands.

You'll meet with a friendly welcome everywhere. Smiles are genuine, humour is jovially sharp. Hospitality is an ancient tradition and nowhere will you find people who are

Dunnottar Castle, setting for Zeffirelli's *Hamlet*

more courteous, or more willing to go out of their way for you. Scots have a reputation for tight-fistedness but generosity among friends and strangers is much more common. Scots have a great respect for education – by the 17th century Scotland had four universities while England still had only two. Most Scots are highly articulate, and will express an independent view on just about every issue, especially political ones.

Scotland is famous for golf, but the one subject that's certain to fire the hearts of most Scotsmen is football, with the rivalry between two Glasgow teams, Rangers and Celtic, inspiring passionate debate. The national team also arouses fierce loyalties.

Religious observance is still a factor in the Highlands and Islands, but elsewhere the former blue laws that once kept

Kilts and Tartans

Brightly coloured tartan kilts have been worn in the Highlands since the Middle Ages but most of the tartans we see today date from the early 19th century when the British royal family made the Highlands fashionable. Daytime Highland dress consists of a knee-length kilt, matching waistcoat and tweed jacket, long knitted socks (with a sgian dubh stuck in the right stocking), and flashes. A sporran (purse) hangs from the waist, and a plaid (sort of tartan rug) is sometimes flung over the shoulder.

The Clearances in the aftermath of the Battle of Culloden in 1746 destroyed the clan system and Highland dress was forbidden. The kilt survived only because the Highland regiments, recruited to help defeat Napoleon, were allowed to continue to wear it. Authentic tartans are registered designs, and each clan has its own pattern. As the clans subdivided, many variations (setts) were produced. Today, there are some 2,500 designs in all. To find out more, visit the Edinburgh Old Town Weaving Company at 555 Castlehill, Edinburgh (open daily).

everything closed down on Sunday are giving way. In the cities you will now find a full range of shopping and entertainment on Sundays, though in the smaller towns the shops may be closed. The Scots do live up to their reputation for enjoying a drink or two and the consequential high level of alcoholism is an acknowledged problem. Heart disease is another worry, with a national diet that is low in fresh fruit and vegetables but high in fat, though things are beginning to change.

Highland dress at the Games

True Grit

Over the centuries the hard-working Scots have made their mark on all corners of the globe: they were frontiersmen in North America, explorers in Africa, pioneers in Australia. Nowadays about ten times as many people of Scottish birth or ancestry live abroad as at home. Intellectually, the contribution made by Scots to world science, medicine and industry has been little short of astonishing. Above all, what binds the Scots together is a love of country plus a strong sense of community and national identity.

All over Scotland you will see and hear the exhortation to 'Haste ye back' ('Come back soon'). After sampling the extraordinary beauty and diversity of this delightful country, you'll want to do just that.

A BRIEF HISTORY

Scotland's earliest settlers are thought to have been Celtic-Iberians who worked their way up from the Mediterranean – they have left us evidence of their presence in the cairns and standing stones which are found all over the country. In recent years, archaeologists discovered the remains of a huge timbered building west of Aberdeen which pre-dates Stonehenge by 1,000 years.

By the time the Romans invaded Scotland in AD84, the inhabitants of the northern region were the Picts, whom they dubbed 'the painted people'. The Roman legions defeated the Picts but were spread too thin to hold 'Caledonia', as they called the area. They withdrew behind the line of Hadrian's Wall, close to and south of the present Scottish-English border. The Picts left little evidence of their culture or language.

Christianity and the Norse Invasion

A Gaelic-speaking tribe from Ireland, the Scots founded a shaky kingdom in Argyll known as 'Dalriada'. In the late 4th century a Scot, St Ninian, travelled to Rome and, on his return, introduced Christianity to Dalriada. His colleague, St Mungo, established the foundation that is now the Cathedral of Glasgow. However, Christianity remained fairly isolated until the arrival in 563 of the great missionary from Ireland, St Columba. For more than 30 years, from the remote island of Iona, he spread the faith that would eventually provide the basis for the unification of Scotland. Tiny Iona today remains one of the most venerated sites in Christendom.

In the late 8th century the Vikings swarmed over Europe setting up strongholds in the Orkneys and Hebrides and on the northern mainland. The Norsemen were to hold the Western Islands, Orkney and the Shetlands for hundreds of years.

Unification and Feudalism in the South

The unifying influence of Christianity allowed an early chieftain, Kenneth MacAlpin, to unite the Scots and the Picts in 843. In 1018 this kingdom, led by Malcolm II, defeated the Northumbrians from the south at the Battle of Carham and extended its domain to the present southern boundary of Scotland. The 'murder most foul' of Malcolm's grandson, Duncan II, by Macbeth of Moray was the inspiration for Shakespeare's Scottish tragedy.

Malcolm III, also known as Malcolm Canmore, changed the course of Scottish history when he married an English princess in 1069. This was the highly pious Queen Margaret who was later canonised. She brought a powerful English influence to the Scottish scene and sought to implement a radical change, replacing the Gaelic-speaking culture of Scotland and its Celtic church with the English-speaking culture and institutions of the south and the church of Rome.

St Margaret's Chapel,
Edinburgh Castle

The rift that Margaret created was widened by her son, David I (reigned 1124–53). He embarked on a huge building programme, founding the great abbeys of Melrose and Jedburgh. He also brought Norman influence into Scotland and introduced to the Lowlands a French-speaking aristocracy and a feudal system of land ownership based on the Anglo-Norman model. He was not successful, however, in imposing this system on the north, where the social structure was based on kinship and where the clan chieftain held land, not for himself, but for his people.

The Shaping of Scotland

The death of King Alexander III (1249–86) in a riding accident touched off a succession crisis that began what was to be the long, bloody struggle for Scottish independence. The English king, Edward I, was invited to arbitrate among the claimants to the throne. He seized his opportunity and installed John Balliol as his vassal king of Scots. But in 1295 Balliol renounced his fealty to Edward and allied himself with France. In retaliation the English king sacked the burgh of Berwick, crushed the Scots at Dunbar, swept north, seized the great castles and took from Scone Palace the Sacred Stone of Destiny on which all Scottish monarchs had been crowned. Edward had earned his title 'Hammer

William Wallace

After a comparatively peaceful interlude, England's insidious interference provoked a serious backlash in 1297. William Wallace, a violent youth from Elderslie, became an outlaw after a scuffle with English soldiers in which a girl (some think she was his wife) who helped him escape was killed herself by the Sheriff of Lanark. Wallace returned to kill the sheriff, but didn't stop there; soon he had raised enough of an army to drive back the English, making him for some months master of southern Scotland. But Wallace wasn't supported by the nobles, who considered him low-born and, after being defeated at Falkirk by England's Edward I, he was hanged, drawn and quartered. His quarters were sent to Newcastle, Berwick, Stirling and Perth.

William Wallace rallies his Scottish forces against the English

of the Scots'. Scotland seemed crushed. However, one man, William Wallace, rose up and led a revolt, soundly defeating the English at Stirling Bridge. Edward responded by routing Wallace at Falkirk. In 1305, Wallace was captured, taken to London and brutally executed.

Robert the Bruce then took up the cause. After he was crowned king at Scone in 1306, he was forced to flee to Ireland. The story goes that when he was most discouraged, he watched a spider spinning a web and, inspired by this example of perseverance and courage, he resolved never to give up hope. The next year he returned to Scotland and captured Perth and Edinburgh. In 1314 at Bannockburn, he faced an army that outnumbered his forces three to one and had superior weapons. However, Bruce had chosen his ground and his strategy skilfully and won a decisive victory. Bruce continued to hammer away at the English until 1328, when Edward III signed a treaty recognising the independence of

Scotland. Robert the Bruce died the following year, honoured as Scotland's saviour.

The Stewarts

In 1371 the reign of the Stewart, or Stuart, dynasty began. While the family was intelligent and talented, it seemed also prone to tragedy. The first three kings all came to power while still children; James I, II and II all died relatively young in tragic circumstances. James IV, who ruled 1488–1513, was an able king who quashed the rebellious Macdonald clan chiefs who had been styling themselves 'Lords of the Isles' since the mid-14th century. In 1513 there was disaster: to honour the 'auld alliance' with France, James led his Scottish troops in an invasion over the English border. In the Battle of Flodden that followed, the Scots were crushed by the English in their worst ever defeat. About 10,000 lost their lives, including the king himself and most of the peerage. One result of the battle was to bring infant James V to the throne. His French second wife, Mary of Guise-Lorraine was the mother of Mary, Queen of Scots. James died prematurely in 1542, six days after his wife had given birth to his heir.

The Apprentice Pillar in the 15th-century Rosslyn Chapel

Mary, Queen of Scots

The tragic events of this queen's life have captivated the imagination of generations. After the infant Mary was crowned, Henry VIII tried to force the betrothal of Mary to his son, Edward and thus unite the two crowns. At the age of five

Mary was sent to France for safekeeping. Her pro-Catholic mother, supported by French forces, took over as regent, a move that was not popular with most Scots.

At the age of 15, Mary was married to the heir to the French throne. He died soon after becoming king, however, and in 1561 Mary, a devout young Catholic widow, returned to Scotland to assume her throne. There she found the Protestant Reformation in full swing, led by John Knox. A follower of Geneva Protestant John Calvin, Knox was a bitter enemy of both the Roman Catholic and the Anglican Church. Mary's agenda was bound to cause trouble: to restore Roman Catholicism and to rule as queen of Scotland in the French style. The Scottish monarchs had been kings of the Scots, not of Scotland so they were answerable to the people – a fundamental difference. She alienated the lords who held the real power and came into conflict with Knox, who heaped insults on her in public.

Mary spent just six turbulent years as Scotland's queen. Scandals surrounded her. In 1565 she married Henry, Lord Darnley and the next year bore a son, the future James VI. Darnley was implicated in the murder of Mary's confidential secretary at Holyroodhouse. Darnley himself was murdered two years later and many suspected Mary's involvement. Doubts crystallised when, a few months later,

Mary, Queen of Scots

she married one of the plot's ringleaders, the Earl of Bothwell. Deposed and held captive, she made a daring escape to England, there to become a thorn in the side of her cousin, Elizabeth I and a rallying point for Catholic dissidents. Mary was kept in captivity in England for nearly 20 years until, in 1587, she was finally beheaded.

Towards Union with England

After his mother's death, James VI assumed the throne as Scotland's first Protestant king. When Elizabeth died in 1603, James rode south to claim the English throne as James I. But the Union of Crowns did not bring instant harmony. The 17th century witnessed fierce religious and political struggles in Scotland. James and his son Charles I (1625–49) had to face opposition from Scottish churchmen. In 1638 Scots signed the National Covenant, giving them the right to their own form of Presbyterian worship.

When the civil war broke out in England, the Covenanters at first backed Parliament against Charles. After he was beheaded in 1649, the Scots backed Charles II. However, Presbyterianism was not formally established as the Church of Scotland until Catholic James VII (James II of England) was deposed in the Glorious Revolution of 1688, which brought Protestant joint monarchs, William III and Mary II of Orange to the English throne (1689–1702). In 1707, despite widespread Scottish opposition, England and Scotland signed the Act of Union. The Scots were to have minority representation in the upper and lower houses at Westminster, they were to keep their own courts and legal system and the status of the national Presbyterian Church was guaranteed. But Scottish nationalism was not so easily subdued.

The Jacobites

Four times in the next 40 years the Jacobites tried to restore the exiled royal family to the throne. The most serious effort was the Rising Stewart, known as 'Bonnie Prince Charlie'. This grandson of James VII was 24 years old when he sailed from France disguised as a divinity student to land in Scotland in July 1745. Within two months he had rallied enough clan support to occupy Perth and Edinburgh. In early November he invaded England, pushing to Derby by 4 December.

Bonnie Prince Charlie

However, English Jacobites failed to come to the aid of the rebellion and again, no help appeared from France. Charles' troops were hopelessly outnumbered. Reluctantly he agreed to retreat north and, by 20 December, they were back in Scotland. From this time on, the Jacobite cause went downhill. The final blow came at the Battle of Culloden Moor which was fought near Inverness on 16 April

1746. The weary Highlanders were subjected to a crushing defeat at the hands of superior government forces under the Duke of Cumberland. In less than an hour, about 1,200 of Charles's men were killed; many others, wounded and captured, were treated in a brutal manner that earned Cumberland the lasting sobriquet of 'Butcher'. Charles escaped, aided by Flora MacDonald, who became Scotland's romantic heroine. After spending five months as a fugitive in the Highlands and Western Isles, he left his country for good aboard a French ship.

The Aftermath

Although the Jacobite cause was finished, Highlanders had to face harsh consequences. The clan structure was destroyed, Gaelic suppressed and wearing of the kilt or plaid was banned. Clans who had supported the rebellion lost their lands. Thousands of crofters (farmers of smallholdings) had to abandon their homes to wealthy sheep farmers from the south under the Highland Clearances programme. Many emigrated to the United States and Canada. Today the Highland glens still remain empty.

Stewart standard

Bonnie Prince Charlie arrived at Glenfinnan on 19 August 1745 and raised the Stewart standard. He rallied 1,200 clansmen ready to battle for the British throne. Seventy years later, Alexander MacDonald of Glenaladale built the Glenfinnan Memorial in memory of all the clansmen who had fought for the cause.

While the Highlands were emptying, the less troubled part of Scotland was booming. Glasgow's tobacco monopoly enriched its merchants and James Watt's invention of the steam engine made the Industrial Revolution possible. Glasgow, with its famous shipbuilding industry, became the 'Workshop of the Empire'. Edinburgh began development into an international

Bonnie Prince Charlie raised the Stewart standard at Glenfinnan

intellectual and cultural centre. The so-called 'Scottish Enlightenment' produced philosophers like David Hume and poets like Robert Burns.

Unlike England, with its rigid class system, Scotland's more democratic attitude made it far easier for poor boys to gain a university education. The work of Scottish scientists, writers, explorers, engineers and industrialists became famous worldwide. In the 1860s Queen Victoria and Prince Albert discovered the Highlands and made tartan apparel fashionable by adopting it themselves.

Yet with the political centre in Westminster and a system in place that gave precedence to English affairs, Scotland was never an equal partner in the union with England. During the privations of the Great Depression and the industrial downturn after World War II, Scots felt impotent and apathetic. But when North Sea oil was discovered, the failing Scottish economy did a turnaround, and with the new prosperity came a resurgence of Scottish national spirit.

Modern Scotland

In 1997 the Scots voted overwhelmingly for the re-establishment of a Scottish Parliament. The new Scottish Parliament, opened in 1999, has control over all local affairs, such as education, economic development, agriculture and the environment, but maintains only a limited ability to collect and control tax revenues. Nonetheless, many Scots see this as a new beginning, a chance to assert their national identity and protect their culture and heritage. A state-of-the-art new Scottish Parliament building – way over budget and well past its original completion deadline – opened for business at Holyrood in 2004.

Scottish history has been deeply emeshed with that of Great Britain for over 300 years but plans for further independence from Westminster have been in place since the 2007 election, when the Scottish National Party gained power by a one-seat majority. Its leader, Alex Salmond, is firmly installed as First Minister of the country.

Scottish Parliament building

The launch of Independence 2010 Scotland had hoped to bring a referendum for the future of an independent Scotland. However, the idea was dropped due to lack of parliamentary support, and superseded by Westminster's new Scotland Bill. This will bring further devolution to the Scottish Parliament through new budget and fiscal powers.

Historical Landmarks

c. 6000BC First signs of human settlement in Scotland.

AD84 Romans beat the 'Caledonians' in the Battle of Mons Graupius.

AD185 Romans withdraw behind the line marked by Hadrian's Wall.

5th century Gaelic-speaking 'Scots' enter the country from Ireland.

563 St Columba spreads Christianity in Scotland.

775–800 Norse forces occupy Hebrides, Orkney and Shetland.

843 Kenneth MacAlpin becomes the first King of the Scots.

1249–86 King Alexander III's reign marks a Golden Age for Scotland.

1290 A succession crisis allows Edward I of England to seize control.

1296 The Sacred Stone of Destiny is removed to London.

1297 William Wallace leads a revolt.

1305 Wallace taken to London and executed.

1306–28 Robert the Bruce wins independence back for Scotland.

1371 Reign of the Stewart dynasty begins.

1513 Defeat to the English in the Battle of Flodden, King James IV killed.

1542 Mary, Queen of Scots crowned at just six days old.

1561 Mary returns to Scotland from France to assume her throne.

1568 Mary flees to England, where she is imprisoned.

1587 Mary is beheaded in England.

1603 James VI, Mary's son, unites the thrones as James I of England.

1638 National Covenant signed, starting a long period of rebellion.

1692 The MacDonalds are massacred at Glen Coe by the Campbells.

1707 Act of Union between England and Scotland.

1745 'Bonnie Prince Charlie' takes back Scotland and invades England.

1750–1800 'Scottish Enlightenment'.

1765 James Watt invents the steam engine.

1780 Crofters lose their land in the Highland Clearances programme.

1997 Referendum votes in favour of separate Scottish Parliament.

2004 New Scottish Parliament building opened.

2007 Alex Salmond (SNP) is elected First Minister of Scotland.

2010 The new Scotland Bill promises further devolution to the Scottish parliament.

WHERE TO GO

Scotland's spectacular and varied scenery and rich historical heritage make it a fascinating country to explore. The country is about 565km (350 miles) from north to south and stretches in some parts as wide as 258km (160 miles), not counting the many islands of the Inner and Outer Hebrides. It is best to concentrate on a few areas, unless your time is unlimited. Scotland has a good network of roads in the Border country and motorways connecting major cities; however, the many winding roads in central Scotland and the single-lane roads in the Highlands can be slow going *(see page 118)*. It's easy to explore Scotland via its excellent bus system *(see page 132)* or on one of the many tours to places of interest *(see pages 122–3)*.

In a country so rich in sights and experiences, only a selection can be presented below, but you'll find worthwhile sights, unspoiled villages, and spectacular scenery wherever you go, as well as plenty of chances for outdoor sports and adventure.

EDINBURGH

The ancient, proud capital of Scotland is, of course, at its most lively during the Edinburgh Festival in August, but all year round it provides many sights and entertainments to enjoy – particularly when the sun is shining. Both the Old Town up against the rock of Edinburgh Castle and the New Town across the way are full of impressive architecture. And you'll find a remarkably congenial atmosphere – an unexpected bonus in a city of just under half a million people.

Edinburgh's seven hills look northward over the great Firth of Forth estuary or southward to gentle green coun-

Loch Ba in the Inner Hebrides

tryside that rises into hills. Tour guides boast that Edinburgh is probably 1,500 years old and certainly it has been the capital of Scotland since 1437.

Despite all the echoes of the past, the city today seems decidedly young and vibrant. Most of the city's principal sights are within easy walking distance of each other or can be reached by public bus.

Edinburgh Castle

Edinburgh's landmark and Scotland's most popular tourist attraction stands on an extinct volcano, high above the city. It is not known exactly how long ago the history of this great rock began, but there is archaeological evidence that there was human habitation here as early as the 9th century BC. A stone fortification was definitely erected late in the 6th century AD and the first proper castle was built in the 11th century.

The sun rises on the city of Edinburgh

A The entrance to **Edinburgh Castle** (daily 9.30am–6pm, until 5pm Oct–Mar; charge; tel: 0131-225 9846, www.edinburghcastle.gov.uk) lies just beyond the Esplanade, which was once a site for the execution of witches, later a parade ground, and is now a car park and site of the famous **Military Tattoo**, performed during the annual **Edinburgh International Festival**.

The famous Military Tattoo

The black naval cannons poking through the ramparts inside the gate have never been fired, but you'll see the cannon that booms out over the city every weekday at one o'clock.

Tiny **St Margaret's Chapel** is the oldest church in use in Scotland. Said to have been built by David I in the early 12th century in honour of his mother, it has survived assaults over the centuries that destroyed the other structures on Castle Rock. The chapel, which has been simply restored with a plain white interior, is kept decorated with flowers by Scotswomen named Margaret. Close by, in a niche overlooking the city, is the Cemetery for Soldiers' Dogs, with the tombs of regimental mascots.

Further up the hill in Palace Yard is the **Great Hall**, claiming the finest hammer-beam ceiling in Britain. Built in 1503, the oak timbers are joined together without a single nail, screw or bolt. It is here that Scotland's Parliament met for a century. In the **State Apartments** is Queen Mary's Room, the very small chamber in which Mary, Queen of Scots gave birth to James VI (later James I of England).

The castle's greatest treasures – the crown, sceptre and sword of Scotland and the Stone of Destiny – are in the **Crown Room**, reached through a series of rooms with displays detailing Scottish history. The rooms are often extremely crowded. On a busy day, more than 10,000 viewers file through here to see the oldest royal regalia in Europe. The gold-and-pearl crown was first used for the coronation of Robert the Bruce in 1306. It was altered in 1540, and Charles II wore it for the last time in 1651. The sword and sceptre were given to James IV by popes Alexander VI and Julius II. The **Stone of Destiny**, on which Scottish monarchs were traditionally crowned, was only returned to Scotland from captivity in Westminster Abbey in 1996; it had been carried away from Scone in 1296 by English king Edward I, as a symbol of his conquest of Scotland (see page 16).

In the back vault of the French prisons is kept **Mons Meg**, a stout cannon that was forged in Mons (hence the name) in the 15th century. The 6.6-ton monster ingloriously blew up 200 years later while firing a salute to the Duke of Albany and York.

Edinburgh Military Tattoo

In 1950 the city established a Military Tattoo at the same time as the Festival. The event features a highly polished show of military marching, pageantry, mock battles and horsemanship, accompanied by the sounds of pipe-and-drum bands from around the world. All this happens nightly (except Sunday) against the backdrop of the magnificently floodlit castle in an arena erected in the Esplanade.

Tickets (which sell out months in advance) can be bought from the ticket office at 33–34 Market Street (behind Waverley Station), or by phoning tel: 0131-225 1188 (credit cards only). They can also be bought online at www.edintattoo.co.uk.

The Royal Mile

The Royal Mile runs along the ridge from Edinburgh Castle downhill to the royal Palace of Holyroodhouse. The **Old Town's** famous thoroughfare, its cobbles now mostly smoothed, is actually about 2km (1¼ miles) long (the Scottish mile was longer than the English). As it descends, the Royal Mile takes five names: Castlehill, Lawnmarket, High Street, Canongate and Abbey Strand.

The Royal Mile

In medieval times, this was Edinburgh's main drag. Enclosed by the city walls, the town grew upwards. Edinburghers delight in recounting how residents of the high tenements and narrow 'wynds' (alleys) used to toss slops from windows after a perfunctory shout of 'Gardyloo!' (the equivalent of 'garde à l'eau'). Today, it is lined with historic buildings, tourist shops, restaurants and pubs.

On Castlehill the **Camera Obscura** at the top of the **Outlook Tower** (daily Apr–June and Sept–Oct 9.30am–6pm, July–Aug 9.30am–7.30pm, Nov–Mar 10am–5pm; charge; www.camera-obscura.co.uk) offers a fascinating 15-minute show – make sure to go when the weather is dry. After climbing the 98 steps to a darkened chamber, you can enjoy living panoramas of the city, projected on to a circular table-screen. From the rooftop you can view the city through telescopes.

Opposite the tower, in the **Scotch Whisky Experience** (daily Sept–May 10am–6pm, June–Aug 9.30am–6.30pm; charge; www.whisky-heritage.co.uk), you will be transported (in a barrel) through the history of Scotland's 'water of life'.

Further along, in James Court, Dr Samuel Johnson once visited his biographer, James Boswell, a native of Edinburgh. In Brodie's Close the popular local story of Deacon Brodie is recalled: a respected city official and carpenter by day, he was a burglar by night (he made wax impressions of his clients' house keys). Finally arrested and condemned, he tried to escape death by wearing a steel collar under his shirt. Unfortunately for him, the gallows, which he himself had designed, worked perfectly. His double life inspired fellow Scot Robert Louis Stevenson to write *Dr Jekyll and Mr Hyde*.

Gladstone's Land (477B Lawnmarket; daily Apr–Oct 10am–5pm, until 6.30pm July–Aug; charge; tel: 0844-493 2120) is a 17thcentury merchant's house, furnished in its original style, with a reconstructed shop booth on the ground floor.

A brief detour down George IV Bridge takes you to the statuette of **Greyfriars Bobby**. This Skye terrier allegedly wait-

St Giles Cathedral

ed by his master's grave in nearby Greyfriars Churchyard for 14 years until dying of old age in 1872. Admiring the dog's fidelity, the authorities made Bobby a freeman of the city.

Across the road in Chambers Street stands the **National Museum of Scotland** (daily 10am–5pm; free; tel: 0131-225 7534; www.nms. ac.uk), incorporating the Royal Museum (1861), which houses an impressive collection of ethnography, archaeology, technology and

The impressive interior of the Royal Musem

the decorative arts. Currently about half of the museum is closed while the Royal Museum building is transformed, but will reopen in all its glory in 2011.

Back along the Royal Mile, **St Giles Cathedral** (May–Sept Mon–Fri 9am–7pm, Sat 9am–5pm, Sun 1–5pm; Oct–Apr Mon–Sat 9am–5pm, Sun 1–5pm; free, but donations suggested), the High Kirk of Scotland, dominates Parliament Square. Its famous tower spire was built in 1495 as a replica of the Scottish crown. The oldest elements of St Giles are the huge 12th-century pillars that support the spire, but there was probably a church on the site since 854. John Knox preached here; he is thought to be buried in the rear graveyard. The soaring Norman interior of St Giles is filled with memorials recalling the great moments of Scottish history. The stained glass in the church dates from 1883 up to modern times. Most beautiful is the **Thistle Chapel**: dating from 1911, it is ornately carved out of Scottish oak. You'll see a stall for the queen and prince-

John Knox House

ly seats for the 16 Knights of the Thistle, Scotland's oldest order of chivalry.

Across the street lie the **City Chambers**, designed by John Adam in the 1750s. Beneath them is Mary King's Close, one of the areas where, until the 18th century, people lived in crowded, unsanitary conditions that aided the spread of plague and disease.

Further down, **John Knox House** (45 High Street; Mon–Sat 10am–6pm, also Sun noon–6pm July–Aug; charge), dating from 1450, is the oldest house in the city. Most interesting is the unchanged top storey with its stencilled beams. It contains an excellent exhibit on the life of John Knox (1513–72), leader of the Scottish Reformation and one of the most important figures in Scottish history *(see page 19)*. It is also home to the **Scottish Storytelling Centre**.

Across the High Street is the **Museum of Childhood** (Mon–Sat 10am–5pm, Sun noon–5pm; free), with a display of children's toys and games through the centuries. At Canongate Tolbooth, the **People's Story** (163 Canongate; Mon–Sat 10am–5pm; Sun during Aug noon–5pm; free) is a social history museum, telling the stories of Edinburgh's ordinary people through reconstructions that capture the sounds, sights and smells of the past. Across the road is the **Museum of Edinburgh** (Mon–Sat 10am–5pm, also Sun noon–5pm in Aug; free).

The royal **Palace of Holyroodhouse** (daily 9.30am–6pm, until 4.30pm Nov–Mar; closed for Royal and State visits;

charge; tel: 0131-556 5100), at the end of the Royal Mile, began life in about 1500 as a mere guest house for the adjacent, now-ruined abbey. It was much expanded and rebuilt in the 17th century. Visiting monarchs have often resided here *(see page 19)*.

The long Picture Gallery showcases many portraits, purportedly of Scottish kings, which were dashed off between 1684–6 by Jacob de Wit the Younger, a Dutchman. In King James' Tower, up a winding inner stairway, are the apartments of Darnley and Mary, Queen of Scots. A plaque marks the spot where the Rizzio, Mary's Italian secretary, was stabbed with a dagger more than 56 times before the queen's eyes.

Above Holyroodhouse looms **Arthur's Seat**; you can climb ◀**F** up to it through Holyrood Park. Back on Holyrood Road, you'll see the **Scottish Parliament building** (opening times ◀**G** daily subject to Parliamentary business; free; www.scottish.

Inside the state-of-the-art Scottish Parliament at Holyrood

Georgian terrace in
Edinburgh's New Town

parliament.uk), a magnificent showpiece designed by the Catalan architect Enric Miralles which opened in 2004 *(see page 24)*. Nearby, also on Holyrood Road, is **Our Dynamic Earth** (Apr–Oct daily 10am–5.30pm, July–Aug until 6pm; Nov–Mar Wed–Sun 10am–5pm; charge; www.dynamicearth.co.uk), a permanent exhibition with displays on the formation and evolution of the planet.

New Town

Until late in the 18th century Edinburgh was confined to the crowded, unhealthy Old Town, along the ridge from the castle or in the wynds beneath the Royal Mile. The population, which numbered about 25,000 in 1700, had nearly tripled by 1767, when James Craig won a planning competition for an extension to the city. With significant help from the noted Robert Adam, he created the **New Town**, a complete complex of Georgian architecture.

At the centre of New Town is Edinburgh's main thoroughfare, bustling **Princes Street**. Between the historic Balmoral Hotel and Waverley Bridge is the three-level Princes Mall, with the tourist information office at street level. **Princes Street Gardens**, the city's green centrepiece, replaced what was once a fetid stretch of water called Nor' Loch. Rising from the gardens is the Gothic spire of the **Scott Monument**, which was erected in 1844 and has a statue of Sir Walter with his dog and statuettes of Scott's literary characters at its base. The gardens' famous **floral clock** is planted with some 24,000 flowers.

A sloping road known as the Mound passes through the gardens. Here, behind the Royal Scottish Academy, is the **National Gallery of Scotland** (daily 10am–5pm, Thur until 7pm; free; www.nationalgalleries.org) a small but distinguished collection. Look for Van Dyck's *Lomellini Family*, Rubens' *The Feast of Herod*, Velázquez's *Old Woman Cooking Eggs*, and four Rembrandt portraits. The English school is represented by Reynolds, Turner and Gainsborough. Don't miss the many paintings by the city's own Henry Raeburn, especially his well-known work, the *Rev. Robert Walker Skating on Duddingston Loch*.

The Scott Monument

At the west end of Princes Street is **Charlotte Square**, the neoclassical centrepiece of the New Town, designed in 1792 by Robert Adam, Scotland's most celebrated architect of the 18th century. The 11 houses on the north side of the square with their symmetrical façades are considered to be his finest work. At No. 7 Charlotte Square, **Georgian House** (daily, Mar and Nov–Dec 11am–3pm, Apr–Oct 10am–5pm; last admission 30 minutes before closing; charge) has been restored in period-style by the National Trust for Scotland. In the dining room

Calton Hill offers panoramic views of the city

is a splendid table setting of Wedgwood and Sheffield, and in the bed-chamber a marvellous medicine chest as well as a 19th-century water closet called 'the receiver'.

The excellent **Scottish National Gallery of Modern Art** (75 Belford Road; daily 10am–5pm, Thur until 7pm; free; www.national galleries.org) is well worth a visit. The gallery has an international collection as well as work by Scottish artists, and also hosts touring exhibits.

Along Inverleith Row extends the 30 hectares (75 acres) of the much-admired **Royal Botanic Garden** (daily from 10am, Nov–Feb closes 4pm, Mar and Oct 6pm, Apr–Sept 7pm; gardens free, greenhouses charge with a huge collection of rhododendrons and a remarkable rock garden, as well as cavernous plant houses.

At the east end of Princes Street is **Calton Hill**, reached via Waterloo Place. In the old City Observatory you can see a slide show, The Edinburgh Experience, and from the top of the Nelson Monument there is a fine panoramic view.

On the waterfront at Leith the **Royal Yacht** *Britannia* (daily Jan–June, Oct–Dec 10am–3.30pm, July–Sept 9.30am–4.30pm; charge; tel: 0131-555 5566; www.royalyachtbritannia.co.uk) is docked.

Excursions in Lothian

From Edinburgh you can take several excursions by bus to points of interest in the countryside. One of the shortest is to the huge **Hopetoun House** near South Queensferry, 10 miles (16km) west of Edinburgh (Easter–Oct daily 10am–5pm; charge; www.hopetoun.co.uk), a fine example of neo-classical 18th-century architecture. The house has fine original furnishings as well as paintings by Dutch and Italian masters and is set in 100 acres (41 hectares) of parkland with herds of red deer. Its gardens were designed in the grand style of Versailles.

Nearby at Linlithgow, overlooking the loch, stand the ruins of **Linlithgow Palace** (daily Apr–Sept 9.30am–5.30pm, Oct–Mar until 4.30pm; charge), which was the birthplace of Mary, Queen of Scots in 1542. James V, Mary's father, gave the fountain in the courtyard to his wife Mary of Guise as a wedding present. The Great Hall measures 94ft (28m) in length and enough of the enormous building still stands for the visitor to imagine what life must have been like here.

Situated alongside is the **Church of St Michael**, one of the best medieval parish churches in Britain and a

Forth Rail Bridge

About 8 miles (13km) west of Edinburgh is one of the Victorian era's greatest engineering feats, the Forth Rail Bridge (see below). Completed in 1890, the bridge comprises three huge cantilevers joined by two suspended spans, for a total length of 4,746ft (1,447m). For many years it was the world's longest bridge.

fine example of the Scottish Decorated style, where a ghost is said to have warned James IV not to fight against England shortly before he and so many Scots were killed at the Battle of Flodden.

Golf courses, beaches, and pleasant villages make East Lothian a popular holiday destination. A pleasant coastal walk connects North Berwick and Gullane Bay. At **Dirleton**, you will find original stone cottages surrounding a large village green beneath a ruined castle. You can take a boat from North Berwick around the Bass Rock where you will see some of the 8,000 gannets which easily outnumber the other inhabitants such as puffins, shags, kittiwakes and cormorants.

Near Seacliff beach are the formidable reddish ruins of 600-year-old **Tantallon Castle** (Apr–Oct daily 9.30am–5.30pm, until 4.30pm Oct, Nov–Mar Sat–Wed 9.30am–4.30pm; charge) high up on a cliff. Queen Victoria visited this fortress of the Black Douglas clan in 1898, and probably peered into the well, cut 89ft (27m) through sheer rock.

② In the Pentland Hills, just south of Edinburgh, **Rosslyn Chapel** (Mon–Sat 9.30am–5pm, Sun noon– 4.45pm; charge;

The Apprentice

Contained within the small, 15th-century Rosslyn Chapel is the most elaborate stone carving in Scotland. The Seven Deadly Sins, the Seven Cardinal Virtues and a dance of death are extravagantly represented in bas-relief, although interest tends to focus on the Apprentice Pillar with its intricate and abundant flowers and foliage.

The story has never been authenticated, but the pillar is said to have been carved by an apprentice while his master was away. The work was so fine that the master, on his return, flew into a jealous rage and killed the apprentice. Three carved heads at the end of the nave are alleged to depict the unfortunate youth, his grieving mother and his master.

www.rosslynchapel.org.uk) in Roslin, Midlothian, is an un-usual church. Built in 1446, it is richly decorated with carvings both pagan and Christian – biblical stories, 'green men', references to the Knights Templar, and plants of the New World that pre-date Columbus's voyage of discovery.

SOUTHERN SCOTLAND

The many ruined castles and abbeys bear silent witness to the turbulent history of the Borders and Galloway area – centuries of conflict between the Scots and the English and also between Scots and Scots. Today this is a region of peaceful countryside, packed with literary associations, with historic houses, tranquil rivers and attractive market towns.

Abbotsford House

The Borders

Rolling green hills, woods and farmland run from Lothian into Scotland's Borders region. The hilly countryside around **Peebles** is worth exploring, particularly the beautiful Manor Valley. Nearby there are two quite outstanding gardens: **Kailzie Gardens** (on B7062 southeast of Peebles) and **Dawyck Botanic Gardens** (on B712 southwest).

To the east along the River Tweed, near Innerleithen, is **Traquair House** (daily Apr–

Melrose Abbey

The destruction caused by Edward II's attack on Melrose Abbey in 1322 prompted Robert the Bruce to fund the abbey's restoration. His heart is said to be buried near the abbey's high altar, but subsequent excavations have failed to locate any trace of it.

May and Sept noon–5pm, June–Aug 10.30am–5pm, Oct 11am–4pm, Nov Sat–Sun only 11am–3pm; charge; www.traquair.co.uk), dating back some 1,000 years. In all, 27 Scottish and English kings have stayed here. It also sheltered Catholic priests and supporters of the Jacobite cause, and is full of curiosities like a secret stairway to a priest's room and a 14th-century hand-printed bible. It is the oldest inhabited house in Scotland.

Abbotsford House (Apr–May and Oct Mon–Sat 9.30am–5pm, Sun 2–5pm, June–Sept daily 9.30am–5pm; charge; www.scottsabbotsford.co.uk), futher down the Tweed, past Galashiels, was the home of **Sir Walter Scott**. He spent the last 20 years of his life here, writing frantically in an effort to pay his debts. Visitors may inspect rooms containing his personal belongings and collection of arms and armour.

The Border Abbeys

The **Border abbeys** were all founded in the 12th century during the reign of David I. Scotland's four great southern monasteries stand in varying degrees of ruin today. All are worth a visit. Always vulnerable to invading forces from England, the abbeys endured frequent sacking, restoration, then new destruction, again and again.

The impressive ruins of **Melrose Abbey** (daily 9.30am–5.30pm, Oct–Mar until 4.30pm; charge;), built of rose-coloured stone, are set off by close-trimmed lawns. You can still see part of the original, high-arching stone church. You will find a small visitor centre and a museum crowded with relics opposite the entrance.

Kelso Abbey was founded in 1128 and took 84 years to complete. Just one arcaded transept tower and a façade are all that remain to suggest the original dimensions of the oldest and once the richest southern Scottish monastery.

Closer to the English border on the River Tweed, **Jedburgh Abbey** (daily 9.30am–5.30pm, Oct–Mar until 4.30pm; charge) is a more complete structure. The main aisle of the church, which is lined by a three-tiered series of nine arches, is nearly intact. There is an informative visitor centre and a museum. Also in Jedburgh is **Mary, Queen of Scots' House** (Mar–Nov Mon–Sat 10am–4.30pm, Sun 11.30am–4.30pm; charge). Built around 1500 it was named after the queen following a visit in 1566. The museum contains exhibits including the queen's death warrant and a death mask made just after her execution in 1587.

Melrose Abbey ruins

Dryburgh Abbey (daily 9.30am–5.30pm, Oct– Mar until 4.30pm; charge) is probably the most beautiful of the four abbeys, and sits among stately beeches and cedars on the banks of the River Tweed. Some of the monks' cloister survives, but little now remains of the church. The grave of Sir Walter Scott can be found here.

From Bemersyde Hill, which is reached from Dryburgh via Gattonside along a beautiful tree-tunnelled

Robert Burns, the national bard

road (B6356), you can enjoy **Scott's View**, a panorama of the three peaks of the Eildon Hills and the writer Sir Walter Scott's favourite scenic spot.

Ayrshire, Dumfries and Galloway

Ayrshire is **Burns Country**. Robert Burns, the national poet of Scotland, was born in 1759 in Alloway, just south of the thriving coastal town of Ayr, and he lived in this area most of his very full 37 years. Here are all the echoes of his narrative poem 'Tam o'Shanter' and the 'Auld Brig o' Doon' which has spanned the River Doon in Alloway for 700 years. Burns' liking for his wee dram and bonnie lassies seems to have enhanced his already monumental reputation.

In Alloway you can visit the **Burns National Heritage Park** (tel: 01292-443700; www.burnsheritagepark.com), with his carefully preserved birthplace, **Burns Cottage** (daily Apr–Sept 10am–5.30pm, Oct–Mar 10am–5pm; charge). In this whitewashed cottage with a thatched roof you'll see the box bed where Burns and three of his brothers used to sleep as children; even his razor and shaving mirror are displayed. The park has been undergoing major redevelopment, with the **Robert Burns Birthplace Museum** opening in December 2010 (same hours as Burns Cottage; charge).

The nearby Tam O'Shanter Experience is an impressive audio-visual presentation based on Burns' poem about witches. You can follow the **Burns Heritage Trail** down to Dumfries where he died in 1796. The Burns Centre in Dumfries focuses on the years he lived in the town; he is buried in a mausoleum in St Michael's Churchyard.

It is well worth making a detour to visit 17th-century **Drumlanrig Castle** (Apr–Aug daily 11am–4pm; regular guided tours; charge; www.drumlanrig.com) near Thornhill. Of all the priceless treasures in this pink sandstone mansion, you'll linger longest over Rembrandt's *Old Woman Reading* on the main stairway; there are also paintings by Holbein and Gainsborough. Napoleon's dispatch box is also here, a gift from Wellington to the owner of the castle, as well as relics of Bonnie Prince Charlie *(see pages 21–2)*.

South of Dumfries you will find the lovely red sandstone ruins of **Sweetheart Abbey** (Apr–Oct daily 9.30am–5.30pm, until 4.30pm Oct, Nov–Mar Sat–Wed 9.30am–4.30pm; charge), which was founded in the 13th century by

The Brig o' Doon features in Burns' poetry

Gretna Green

Just over the border from England is the small town of Gretna Green, which became celebrated for celebrating marriages. It was the first available community where eloping couples from England could take advantage of Scotland's different marriage laws. Many a makeshift ceremony was performed at the Old Blacksmith's, now a visitor centre, and many romantic couples still choose to be married at Gretna Green today.

the pious (and rich) Devorgilla Balliol, Lady of Galloway. She dedicated it to her husband, John Balliol, who died at a young age and whose embalmed heart she carried around with her in a silver box until her own death in 1289. Also south of Dumfries, do not miss the moated fairytale **Caerlaverock Castle** with red sandstone walls which was built around 1270.

On the other side of the River Nith, **Ruthwell Cross**, named after its hamlet, is kept in a pretty church surrounded by weathered tombstones. This great monument was carved out of brownish-pink stone some 1,300 years ago. Standing 18ft (5.5m) high, it is covered with sculpted figures and runic inscriptions. You may have to ask at a cottage along the lane for the key to the church.

Southwest Scotland has beautiful shorelines, moors and forest scenery. It also claims milder weather than any other area. Just north of Newton Stewart is **Galloway Forest Park**, where you can walk through wild hill country. To the extreme southwest is the peninsula called the Rhinns of Galloway. The **Logan Botanic Garden** (Mar–Oct daily 10am–5pm, Apr–Sept until 6pm; charge) has Scotland's best collection of tree ferns and, among many palms and other warm-weather species, superb magnolias from western China.

At seaside **Port Logan** (pop. 59) with its little yellow houses, three's a crowd at what is probably the smallest post office in Great Britain. It measures about 2 sq yards (1.5 sq m).

From the most southerly point in Scotland, the high-cliffed Mull of Galloway, you can see the Isle of Man on a clear day.

On a pastoral hill midway up the peninsula is a stone chapel which contains several of Scotland's oldest Christian relics: the **Kirkmadrine Stones**, which consist of three stones and various fragments dating back to the 5th century.

Culzean Castle

One of Scotland's top attractions, **Culzean Castle** (daily Mar–Oct 10.30am– 5pm; country park daily all year 9.30am–sunset; charge; tel: 0844-493 2149; www. culzeanexperience. org) towers above the sea on a rugged stretch of the Ayrshire coast. It stands in an estate of over 500 acres (202 hectares) of parkland and stately formal gardens. Now a National Trust property, the castle dates mostly from the late 18th century when it was transformed for the Kennedy family from a 16th-century tower house by the architect Robert Adam. The oval staircase is considered one of Adam's finest designs; the best room is the circular drawing room with its ceiling in three pastel shades, a perfect example of Scottish Enlightenment, its windows overlooking the waves of the Firth of Clyde breaking on the rocks 151ft (46m) below. Upstairs is an exhibition in honour of

Culzean Castle

A tranquil scene on Arran

Dwight D. Eisenhower for his role as Allied Supreme Commander during World War II. In the summer on Sunday afternoons, a pipe band performs on the large sunken lawn of the Fountain Court just below the castle.

Arran

The unspoilt **Isle of Arran** in the Firth of Clyde has been called 'Scotland in miniature'. Car ferries ply regularly between Arran's capital, Brodick, and Ardrossan on the Ayrshire coast; the journey takes 55 minutes. In summer a smaller ferry links northern Arran to Claonaig in Argyll. Brodick village nestles on a bay in the shadow of **Goatfell**, which, at 2,867ft (874m), is the highest peak on Arran. On Brodick Bay, **Brodick Castle** (Easter–Oct Sat–Wed 11am–4pm; country park open daily all year 9.30am–sunset; charge), containing a wealth of treasures, is surrounded by magnificent gardens.

Red deer roam the island's beautiful mountain glens and can often be seen in North Glen Sannox between Lochranza and Sannox. Arran is above all an island for hill walkers or climbers. The most dramatic scenery is in the north of the island. There are ten summits over 2,000ft (610m) and dozens of ridge routes. In the south the topography is gentler, with pleasant hills around the villages of Lamlash and Whiting Bay.

Among the hundred or so species of birds known to frequent Arran are peregrine falcons and rare golden eagles. Seals like the rocks around Arran's 56 miles (90km) of coast. In addition, basking sharks can be seen offshore in the summer.

Arran has some outstanding archaeological sites. There are Neolithic chamber tombs, such as the one at **Torrylinn**, near Lagg, and Bronze Age stone circles around Machrie on the west coast. Towards the island's southwest corner on a wild, cliff-backed coast are the **King's Caves**, where Robert the Bruce is said to have taken refuge in 1307. The caves are a 20-minute walk from the car park.

GLASGOW

Be prepared for a pleasant surprise. In recent years, **Glasgow** 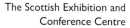 has undergone major changes, and has not only cleaned its splendid Victorian buildings and generally polished up its act, but now proudly presents itself as one of Europe's major centres for culture and the arts. The city is home to the Scottish Opera, Scottish Ballet, the Royal Scottish National Orchestra and the BBC Scottish Symphony Orchestra, and it stages an annual comedy festival in March, as well as a jazz festival in June.

At the heart of Glasgow lies **George Square**, overlooked by the impressive **City Chambers**, opened by Queen Victoria in 1888 (a statue of her on horseback is on the west side of the square). Free tours are given Mon–Fri at 10.30am and

The Scottish Exhibition and Conference Centre

2.30pm. On the south side at No. 11 is a tourist information centre. Glasgow's sophisticated main shopping area is Buchanan Street, which is a block west of George Square.

Traces of Mackintosh

The city is closely connected with Scottish architect **Charles Rennie Mackintosh**. Almost forgotten by his native city at the time of his death, he has become world famous, and today his unique vision is a prominent feature of Glasgow's art scene. The **Glasgow School of Art** (167 Renfew Street; tours given Apr–Sept daily at 10am, 11am, noon, 2pm, 3pm, 4pm and 5pm; Oct–Mar daily 11am and 3pm, reserve tickets in advance; charge), is one of few buildings from his designs built during his lifetime.

Opened in 1996, the **House for an Art Lover** (Bellahouston Park; times can vary, check first; charge www.housefor

The Glasgow Boys

The late-19th and early-20th centuries were a time of artistic ferment in Glasgow, but because of the hide-bound local arts establishment, Glasgow artists often had to look for recognition outside Scotland. Charles Rennie Mackintosh was a leading figure in the Art Nouveau movement on the continent, and influenced designers such as Frank Lloyd Wright as far afield as Chicago, but was not admired at home.

Others who suffered the same fate were painters Sir James Guthrie, Robert MacGregor, William Kennedy, Sir John Lavery and Edward Arthur Walton. After a successful London exhibition, the 'Glasgow School' was born, but the artists always called themselves the 'Glasgow Boys'. More recently, a new generation of Glasgow Boys began to emerge from the School of Art in the 1970s and 1980s. The works of Glasgow Boys of both generations can be seen in the Kelvingrove Art Gallery and the Gallery of Modern Art on Queen Street.

anartlover.co.uk; Art Lover's Café open daily 10am–5pm) was created from a portfolio Mackintosh submitted for a design competition in 1901, following a brief to 'design a house in a thoroughly modern style, where one can be lavishly entertained'.

There is also an exhibit on Mackintosh at **The Lighthouse**, on Mitchell Lane, and the evocative rooms of Mackintosh's own house have been preserved in the  **Hunterian Museum and Art Gallery** at Glasgow

Rodin's *Thinker* in the prestigious Burrell Collection

University (Mon–Sat 9.30am–5pm; gallery free, house charge; www.hunterian.gla.ac.uk). On Sauchiehall Street, stop off at No. 217 for the **Willow Tearoom** (Mon–Sat 9am–5pm, Sun 11am–4.15pm, last orders 30 minutes before closing; tel: 0141-332 0521), a survivor of a series of tearooms designed by the architect. For more information on Mackinstosh attractions in the city contact the Charles Rennie Mackintosh Society (tel: 0141-946 6600; www.crmsociety.com).

Major Museums

Glasgow's most important museum is the **Burrell Collection** (2060 Pollokshaws Road; Mon–Thur and Sat 10am–5pm, Fri and Sun 11am–5pm; free; tel: 0141-287 2550; www.glasgow museums.com) in Pollok Country Park to the southwest of the city centre. Opened in 1983, it holds the thousands of pieces amassed by shipping tycoon Sir William Burrell. The collection has everything from ancient Greek statues to Impressionist paintings, medieval tapestries to stained glass. Also in the park is Pollok House with a fine collection of Spanish art.

In Kelvingrove Park is the city's splendid **Art Gallery and Museum** (Argyle Street; Mon–Thur, Sat 10am–5pm, Fri, Sun 11am–5pm; free; www.glasgowlife.org.uk/museums). On display are a collection of 17th-century Dutch paintings, paintings by Rembrandt, Botticelli, Giorgione and Bellini, as well as an archaeological exhibit, some French Impressionists, 19th-century Scottish paintings and works by the Glasgow Boys.

Also giving a fascinating look into Glasgow's past is the **Tenement House** (145 Buccleuch Street; Mar–Oct daily 1–5pm; charge). Miss Agnes Toward, who lived here from 1911 until 1965, never threw anything away, nor did she ever attempt to modernise the flat; the result is a fascinating glimpse into early 20th-century social history.

Glasgow Cathedral

Old Glasgow

Cathedral Street, located northeast of the city centre, brings you to the city's fine **Cathedral** (Apr–Sept Mon–Sat 9.30am–5.30pm, Sun 1–5.30pm; Oct–Mar Mon–Sat 9.30am–4.30pm, Sun 1–4.30pm; free), the only medieval cathedral in Scotland that has survived intact. Parts of it are almost 800 years old, and it has an unusual two-level construction. The lower church contains the tomb of St Mungo (Kentigern), the city's patron saint. Above the church is the **Necropolis**, filled with the extravagant tombs of the city's late, great Victorians.

Across the street is **Provand's Lordship** (daily Mon–Thur and Sat 10am–5pm, Fri and Sun 11am–5pm; free), the oldest house in Glasgow. Originally, the 15th-century house was home to the cathedral administrative clergy. With its thick stone walls, it is a rare example of Scottish domestic architecture. Opposite is **St Mungo Museum of Religious Life and Art** (Mon–Thur, Sat 10am–5pm, Fri, Sun 11am–5pm; free).

Head south down High Street to London Road to reach **Glasgow Green**, one of the city's many public parks and the oldest in Britain. Here you can learn about the working life of Glaswegians throughout history in the **People's Palace** (Tue–Thur and Sat 10am–5pm, Fri and Sun 11am–5pm; free). The nearby Barras indoor market, open weekends, will give you the chance to rub shoulders with local people and perhaps even pick up a bargain or two.

The Old Docks

More contemporary developments can be seen by the old docks to the west of the city centre. On the north bank of the Clyde is the **Scottish Exhibition and Conference Centre**, its distinctive 'Armadillo' building designed by Sir Norman Foster. Almost opposite, on the south bank, is the stunning, titanium-clad **Glasgow Science Centre** (daily 10am–5pm; charge; www.glasgowsciencecentre.org). This comprises three separate buildings: the Science Mall which contains educational exhibits; the revolving 120-ft (400-m) Glasgow Tower with views as far as Ben Lomond; and an IMAX cinema. To the west, beyond Stobcross Quay and adjacent to Glasgow Harbour, the £74-million futuristic **Riverside Museum** dedicated to transport will open in spring 2011. The Tall Ship, a three-masted Clyde-built barque from 1896, will also be moved here.

CENTRAL SCOTLAND

Stirling

9

With its proud Renaissance castle commanding the major route between the Lowlands and the Highlands, **Stirling** for centuries saw much of Scotland's worst warfare. Guides at the castle regale visitors with tales of sieges, intrigue, dastardly murders and atrocities, and an audio-visual presentation just off the castle esplanade brings the savage saga vividly to life. In contrast to sober Edinburgh Castle, **Stirling Castle** (daily 9.30am–6pm, Oct–Mar until 5pm; charge; tel: 01786-450000; www.stirlingcastle.gov.uk) has a façade covered with all sorts of carvings. Most of the castle dates back about 500 years, though the rock was fortified at least four centuries earlier. The **Palace** was built by James V in Renaissance style, and of interest here are the Stirling Heads, carved roundels that are possibly portraits of members of the court. Mary, Queen of Scots spent her early childhood here, and she was crowned as an infant in the **Chapel Royal**. The **Great Hall**, which faces the upper square, was once the

The Falkirk Wheel

In 2002 Scotland re-asserted itself in the world of engineering by unveiling an iconic landmark, the Falkirk Wheel. Named after the nearby town in central Scotland, the wheel is the world's only rotating boat lift. Built at a cost of over £17 million, the structure connects the Forth and Clyde Canal to the Union Canal, re-establishing the link between Edinburgh and Glasgow. It is part of a larger project to restore the waterways between the east and west coasts.

The site includes a visitor's centre containing a shop, café and exhibition centre (daily Mar–Oct 10am–5.30pm; free, charge for boat trips; www.thefalkirkwheel.co.uk).

greatest medieval chamber in Scotland, suitable for holding sessions of Parliament, but it later suffered through two centuries of use as a military barracks. Restoration has returned it to its original grandeur. The Museum of the Argyll and Sutherland Highlanders contains banners, regimental silver, and artefacts that go back to the Battle of Waterloo. A statue of Robert the Bruce is on the Esplanade.

Seven battlefields can be seen from the castle. In 1297, William Wallace defeated the English at Stirling Bridge. The **Wallace Monument** is at Abbey Craig, east of the town centre. The battlefield of **Bannockburn** is visible to the south of the castle. Here you'll find the Bannockburn Heritage Centre (daily Apr–Sept 10am–5.30pm, Mar, Oct 10am–5pm; charge), where the National Trust presents an audio-visual show explaining the complex wars of independence, which culminated in Robert the Bruce's epic victory over the Eng-

Stirling Castle

lish in 1314. Commemorating this triumph is an equestrian statue of **Robert the Bruce** with the inscription of his declaration: 'We fight not for glory nor for wealth nor for honour, but only and alone we fight for freedom, which no good man surrenders but with his life'.

The medieval **Church of the Holy Rude** (St John Street, Castle Wynd; Easter–Sept 11am–4pm; admission by donation) has a notable medieval hammerbeam oak roof. The infant James VI was crowned here in 1567.

Just north of Stirling, 700-year-old **Dunblane Cathedral** is one of the finest examples of Gothic church architecture in Scotland. It is about a century older than **Doune Castle** (Apr–Oct daily 9.30am–5.30pm, Oct until 4.30pm, Nov–Mar Sat–Wed 9.30am–4.30pm; charge) just to the west. A fortress-residence and once a Stuart stronghold, it is one of the best preserved castles of its period. It has a central courtyard and Great Hall with an open-timbered roof and a minstrel's gallery. Its owner, the Earl of Moray, displays his first-class collection of vintage cars at a nearby museum.

Loch Lomond and the Trossachs

Romantically connected with the legend of Rob Roy, Scotland's folk hero, the **Trossachs** is a region of lovely lochs, glens and bens (mountain peaks), and craggy hills. 'Trossachs' probably means 'bristly places', after the area's wooded crags. Loch Lomond and the Trossachs National Park opened in 2002. Callander is a good centre from which to explore the Trossachs; information is available at the Rob Roy Visitor Centre. You can take a cruise on **Loch Katrine**, the setting of Sir Walter Scott's poem 'The Lady of the Lake', on the Victorian steamer *Sir Walter Scott*, which leaves from Trossachs Pier. Salmon may well be leaping up the easily accessible Falls of Leny below Loch Lubnaig. Between Callander and Aberfoyle, the Duke's Pass has some fine views. To the south is the **Queen Elizabeth Forest Park**, whose woodland walks offer a chance to spot wildlife.

Loch Lomond, the largest freshwater expanse in Great Britain, runs about 24 miles (39km) north to south. Ben Lomond (3,192ft/973m) and companion peaks look down on the sometimes choppy water at the north end of the loch, while to the south the landscape is tranquil and rolling. **Luss** is the prettiest of the little lochside villages. In **Balloch**, stop at the Lomond Shores and National Park Visitor Centre. A number of cruises set sail on Loch Lomond from Balloch, Tarbet, and Luss. The West Highland Way provides a scenic footpath along the east bank of Loch Lomond.

To the west of Loch Lomond at the northern end of Loch Fyne, **Inveraray Castle** (daily Apr–Oct 10am– 5.45pm; charge; www.inveraray-castle.com), with its pointed turrets and Gothic design, contains a wealth of

The bonnie banks of Loch Lomond

treasures. Home of the Dukes of Argyll, it has been the headquarters of Clan Campbell (called 'uncrowned kings of the Highlands') since the 15th century, although the present building dates only from between 1740 and 1790. The impressive interior holds a collection of Regency furniture; Chinese porcelain; portraits by Gainsborough, Ramsey, and Raeburn; and an armoury with an amazing array of broadswords, Highland rifles, and medieval halberds. The guides point out with pride the portrait of the sixth duke, said both to have gambled away a fortune and to have fathered 398 illegitimate children.

 Further south along Loch Fyne are the delightful **Crarae Garden** (open all year round daily 9.30am–sunset; charge), with many unusual plants, such as the Himalayan rhododendrons, and plants from Tasmania and New Zealand. The gardens are at their best in late spring. You can choose from three walks over the 50 acres (20 hectares) of hillside, all within earshot of a plunging brook.

Fife

Dunfermline is dominated by the ruins of the **Abbey and Palace of Dunfermline**. King Malcolm Canmore made Dunfermline his capital around 1060, and his pious queen, St Margaret, founded the Benedictine abbey. Of the great abbey church, only the nave with its massive Norman arches survives. Nearby, the 14th-century **Abbot House** has an interesting historical display. Industrialist and philanthropist **Andrew Carnegie** was born here and his birthplace cottage and museum is open to visitors Mar–Nov Mon–Sat 10am–5pm, Sun 2–5pm; free.

Also in this area is **Culross**, thought to be the birthplace of St Mungo. It is a wonderfully preserved 17th- and 18th-century village restored by the National Trust for Scotland. Among places of historic interest are Bruce's Palace from

1577 and the ruined abbey and Abbey House. The Trust runs a guided tour departing from the palace reception.

The most famous place on the Fife coast is **St Andrews,**
where golf has been played for 500 years. It's possible, if you are an experienced golfer, to tee off on the **Old Course** *(see pages 89–90)*. At the 18th hole is the Royal and Ancient Golf Club, which maintains the rules of the game. This pleasant seaside resort is also home to Scotland's oldest university (founded in 1413); its buildings are dotted all over town. Here also is the ruin of what was Scotland's largest-ever cathedral, an enormous structure built in the 12th and 13th centuries, where the marriage of James V and Mary of Guise took place. Learn more about golf at the **British Golf Museum**; and for culture the local theatre, The Byre, is well-regarded.

The picturesque **East Neuk** fishing villages on Fife's south-eastern coast are more dependent on tourism than fishing

The ruin of St Andrews Cathedral

nowadays. **Crail** is a little port with a Dutch-style tolbooth (court-house jail) and restored buildings: a photographer's delight. **Anstruther** (which the locals pronounce 'Anster'), once the herring capital of Scotland, is worth a stop for the Scottish Fisheries Museum with its realistic fisherman's cottage of about 1900, magnificent ship models, whale tusks, and a display about trawlers. From here you can go to the **Isle of May**, a bird sanctuary with cliffs that measure 249ft (76m). **Pittenweem's** venerable harbour is still the base for what's left of the East Neuk fishing fleet.

Across the Firth of Tay, which is spanned by one of the world's longest railway bridges as well as a road bridge, lies

Lobster pots

Dundee, famous maritime and industrial centre. Docked in the harbour is the Royal Navy's oldest ship, HMS *Unicorn*, and Captain Scott's ship, the RRS *Discovery*, built here at the turn of the 20th century and used in his polar expeditions.

Perth and Scone Palace

Perth was Scotland's medieval capital, and has many reminders of its historic heritage. John Knox preached in the **Church of St John**, founded in 1126, inspiring his followers to destroy many monasteries in the area in 1559. Just 2 miles (3km) north of Perth, the pale red sandstone **Scone Palace**

(Mon–Sat Apr–Oct 9.30am–5.30pm, until 4.30pm Sat); charge; www.scone-palace.net) was built on the site of one of these monasteries. From the 9th to the 13th century, Scone (pronounced 'Scoon') guarded the famous **Stone of Destiny**, on which the kings of the Scots were crowned. Edward I, believing in the symbolic magic of the stone, carried it away in 1296 and took it to London where, until 1996, it rested under the chair on which the English kings were crowned in Westminster Abbey. Romantics, however, believe that the stone, now on display in Edinburgh Castle (see page 30), is not the original stone, but a replica produced by the Scots to fool Edward, and suggest that the real stone (which they think was covered with carvings) is still hidden in Scotland.

Three Js

The industrial history of Dundee is often described by 'the three Js' – jute, jam and journalism. The city's rapid growth in population during the 19th century was due in large part to the jute industry, now completely gone. The only 'J' still thriving is journalism – newspaper and comic publisher D.C. Thomson & Co celebrated its centenary in 2005.

In the palace, the ancestral home of the Earls of Mansfield, are many treasures, including early Sèvres, Derby, and Meissen porcelain, and artefacts such as the embroideries of Mary, Queen of Scots. In the Long Gallery are more than 80 Vernis Martin objects, which look like lacquered porcelain but are in fact papier mâché. This unique collection will never be copied: the Martin brothers died in Paris in the 18th century without disclosing the secret of their varnish. Before leaving Scone, stroll through the grounds to the Pinetum, an imposing collection of California sequoias, cedars, Norway spruces, silver firs, and other conifers in a gorgeous setting.

Perthshire

Glamis Castle (daily Mar–Dec 10am–6pm, last tour 4.30pm; Nov–Dec 10.30am–4.30pm, last tour 3pm; charge) lies northeast of Perth towards Forfar. It was the childhood home of Queen Elizabeth, the late Queen Mother, and the birthplace of the late Princess Margaret. Visitors can take guided tours through the magnificent rooms. On the way to Glamis Castle, enthusiasts of archaeology will want to stop to look at the elaborately carved early-Christian and Pictish monuments in the museum at **Meigle**.

Northwest of Perth is **Dunkeld**, with its restored 'little houses' from the 17th century. They lead to a once grand cathedral, now partly ruined, although the choir of the cathedral was renovated in the 17th century to serve as a parish church. The cathedral stands amid tall trees, lawns, and interesting gravestones beside the River Tay. The site was an ancient centre of Celtic Catholicism, and St Columba is said to have preached in a monastery on this site. Also note Thomas Telford's arched bridge (1809) over the Tay.

Lonely piper at Glamis Castle

Binoculars are provided at a fine wooden hide at the **Loch of the Lowes Wildlife Reserve**, two wooded miles (3km) from Dunkeld. Here you can scan all kinds of water-bird life and study trees where ospreys nest after migrating from Africa.

At the hamlet of Meikleour, one of the arborial wonders of the world lines the road: a gigantic **beech hedge**, which at about 89ft (27m) is the highest anywhere, planted in 1746 and still thriving.

Near Aberfeldy, once a Pictish centre, is the delightful little village of Fortingall on Loch Tay, with probably Scotland's finest thatched-roof cot-

Pitlochry

tages. It boasts the 'oldest living tree' in Europe, the **Fortingall Yew**. This ancient yew tree, surrounded by a rusty iron and stone enclosure in Fortingall's churchyard, is still growing and certainly doesn't look its presumed age – 3,000 years. The hamlet is in Glen Lyon, the 'longest, loveliest, loneliest' glen in Scotland, according to the locals. Tranquillity reigns. Tradition has it – without scholarly confirmation – that Pontius Pilate was born in a nearby military encampment while his father was a Roman emissary to the Pictish king in the area.

Centrally located, the crowded summer resort of **Pitlochry** is surrounded by dozens of attractions, both scenic and manmade. In the town itself, you might visit the Pitlochry Dam and Fish Pass, where each year about 5,500 salmon are counted electronically and watched through a windowed chamber as they make their way towards their spawning grounds. Pitlochry also has a **Festival Theatre**.

A short drive west will bring you to the **Pass of Kil-**

liecrankie, where you will want to walk along wooded paths to the spectacular parts of the gorge. A National Trust centre here describes a particularly bloody battle between Jacobite and government forces in 1689. Just south, a roadside promontory known as the **Queen's View** commands a glorious sweep down along Loch Tummel and over Highland hills. On a good day this is among the best panoramas in Scotland.

North of Killekrankie, the white-turreted **Blair Castle** (Apr–Oct daily 9.30am–5.30pm; charge; www.blair-castle. co.uk), seat of the Earls and Dukes of Atholl, is a major tourist destination. The present duke commands Britain's only 'private army', a ceremonial Highland regiment of about 60 local riflemen and 20 pipers and drummers who march in their regalia very occasionally. Part of the castle dates back 700 years, but it has been much reconstructed

Blair Castle, seat of the Earls and Dukes of Atholl

and restored. It's crammed with possessions amassed by the Atholl family over the centuries: an extensive china collection, swords, rifles, antlers, stuffed animals and portraits. Look in particular for two rare colonial American powder horns, one with a map carved on it that shows forts and settlements around Manhattan island, Albany, and the Mohawk River.

Further west from Pitlochry is the long and thickly forested **Glen Garry**, one of Scotland's most wonderful mountain valleys. Be sure not to miss the **Falls of Bruar** cascading into the River Garry near the lower end of the glen.

Aberdeen

The term 'granite city' is self-explanatory when you see the buildings sparkling in the sunshine at **Aberdeen**. Surprisingly, however, this solid metropolis, further north than Moscow, is anything but sombre: roses, daffodils and crocuses flourish in such profusion that the town has repeatedly won the Britain-in-Bloom trophy. You will find Aberdeen's excellent tourist information centre at St Nicholas House on Broad Street.

Scotland's third city is Europe's offshore oil capital, and one of Britain's major fishing ports. For the best show in town, don't fail to make an early-morning visit (before 7.30am) to the huge harbourside **fish market**. Containers of fish by the thousand are unloaded from the weathered trawlers. There are huge triangular halibut, long black-grey 'coaleys' (coalfish), gigantic skate, greyish-white ling, dogfish, turbot, whiting, cod and haddock.

The traditional fishing industry still has a role to play in the economic life of the city, but most of the boats arriving in the harbour service the great oil rigs and platforms out at sea beyond the horizon. Aberdeen is Scotland's boom city, and its facilities have expanded to accommodate the influx of North Sea oil personnel, creating something of an international atmosphere for the many tourists who visit in the summer.

In the heart of the town, **Marischal College** is the second-largest granite building in the world after the Escorial in Spain. Built of a lighter-coloured variety known as 'white granite', it forms part of the complex of Aberdeen University. The city's first university, King's College, was founded in 1495. Dominating the pleasant quadrangle is the beloved local landmark, the Crown Tower of **King's Chapel**. Knocked down in a storm in 1633, the structure was rebuilt with Renaissance additions. Inside the chapel, look for the arched oak ceiling, carved screen and stalls and Douglas Strachan's modern stained-glass windows.

Nearby is the crowded graveyard of the oldest cathedral in Aberdeen, **St Machar's Cathedral**, first built in 1357, and

Aberdeen's harbour

rebuilt in granite in the 15th century. It is the oldest granite building in the city. Capping the marvellous stone interior with its stained-glass windows is a wonderful oak ceiling, bearing seals of kings and religious leaders.

One of Aberdeen's most interesting sites is **Provost Skene's House** (Guestrow, off Broad Street; Mon–Sat 10am–5pm; free), which was

Aberdeen, the granite city

built in 1545 is among the oldest houses in Aberdeen. Its rooms span 200 years of period design. In the Painted Gallery is an important cycle of religious art, painted by an unknown 17th-century artist.

The 17th-century **Mercat Cross**, which is ringed by a parapet on which are engraved the names of Scottish monarchs from James I to James VII, is claimed to be the finest example of a burgh (chartered town) cross to survive in Scotland. Aberdeen's charter dates back to 1179.

Dunnottar Castle

South of Aberdeen, near Stonehaven, the vast ruins of **Dunnottar Castle** rise above the sea. The fortress has had a rich and varied history. Here, in 1297, William Wallace burned alive an English Plantagenet garrison. Much later, in 1650, the Scottish Crown Regalia were kept here during a siege by Oliver Cromwell's Roundheads. More recently, not to mention more peacefully, the film director Franco Zeffirelli used Dunnottar as the location for his film of Hamlet. Note: the steep steps down to the castle may be difficult for less mobile visitors.

Royal Deeside

The long, picturesque valley of the River Dee, extending inland from Aberdeen to the high Cairngorm Mountains, has been called **Royal Deeside** since Queen Victoria wrote glowingly about the area. Her 'dear paradise', **Balmoral Castle**, was purchased by Prince Albert in 1852. He refashioned the turreted mansion to his own taste in the Scottish Baronial style; the granite is local, and lighter than Aberdeen's. Balmoral is about 41 miles (66km) west of Aberdeen. If the royal family is not in residence, the grounds are open daily to the public (late Apr–July 10am–5pm; charge; www.balmoralcastle.com). Across the road, modest Crathie Church is attended by the royal family.

Dunnottar Castle

Along the Dee near Aberdeen, **Crathes Castle** (June–Aug daily 10.30am–5pm, Apr–May, Sept–Oct Sat–Thur 10.30am–4.30pm, Nov–Mar Sat–Sun 10.30am–3.45pm; garden daily 9am–sunset; charge) has some of Scotland's most dramatic gardens, with giant yew hedges that are clipped just once a year. The views from within the 16th-century tower-house over these remarkable hedges are in themselves worth the visit. Look also for the three rooms with painted ceilings, the carved-oak ceiling in the top-floor gallery, and the 14th-century ivory Horn of Leys, above the drawing-room fireplace.

THE HIGHLANDS

No longer really remote, the sparsely populated north of Scotland offers, above all, superb scenery as well as the country's most mysterious monster and most important distilleries.

The River Spey and the Malt Whisky Trail

For salmon and whisky, Scotland can offer you nothing better than the **River Spey**. Along this beautiful valley of ferns and old bridges, you'll want to stop to watch anglers casting their long lines into this fastest-flowing river in the British Isles. Nestling among the trees are slate-roofed buildings with pagoda chimneys. Here they produce the finest of all the fine Scotch whiskies, or so the local enthusiasts insist.

The Malt Whisky Trail, www.maltwhiskytrail.com, takes in seven distilleries where you can watch malt being distilled by a process that has remained basically unchanged for 500 years. You will usually be invited to enjoy a free wee dram. Contact the local tourist offices to check when the distilleries accommodate visitors and when they're closed (annual shutdowns last up to six weeks, sometimes in July or August). If you're lucky, at the Speyside Cooperage (Mon–Fri 9am–4pm; charge) you'll see a cooper (cask maker) fashioning oak staves into a cask: by law a spirit can't be called 'whisky' until it has been aged in oak for three years. According to the experts, the best maturity for Scotch is about ten years.

Around the malt centre of Dufftown they still like to quote the saying: 'Rome was built on seven hills, Dufftown stands on seven stills' – although at a recent count there were in fact eight distilleries. Some distilleries to visit are **Cardhu Distillery** in Knockando, **Glenfarclas** in Ballinalloch, **Glenfiddich** in Dufftown, **Glen Grant** in Rothes, **Glenlivet** in Glenlivet, and **Strathisla** in Keith.

The Northeast Coast and Inverness

The northeast coast consists of a fertile coastal plain, shielded to the south by the Cairngorm Mountains. In the 19th century, this area was the centre of a fishing industry, and is dotted with many attractive fishing towns and villages, such as Buckie, Cullen and Portsoy. Just south of Lossiemouth, a fine fishing town and port, lies Elgin, a picturesque town that retains much of its medieval layout, with a cobbled marketplace and winding streets. The 13th-century **Elgin Cathedral** was once known as the 'Lantern of the North', and its ruins are still impressive.

16 ▸ In the Highlands, all roads lead to **Inverness**, capital of the Highlands since the days of the ancient Picts. It is worth stopping in this busy town to tour the small, modern **Museum and Art Gallery** (Castle Wynd; Mon–Sat 9am–5pm; www.invernessmuseum.com; free). In a fascinating exhibition of Scottish Highland history dating back to the Stone Age, you can brush up on your clan lore as well as inspect the dirks and sporrans, broadswords, and powder horns.

Urquhart Castle

Urquhart Castle (daily Apr–Oct 9.30am–6pm, Nov–Mar until 4.30; charge) sits by Loch Ness between Fort William and Inverness. Dating back to the 13th century, the castle played a key role in the Wars of Independence, being taken by Edward I and later by Robert the Bruce. Part of the building was blown up in 1692 to prevent it falling into Jacobite hands.

Loch Ness

Strategically situated where the River Ness joins the Moray Firth, **Inverness** is not at all shy about exploiting the submarine celebrity presumed to inhabit the waters of **Loch Ness** to the ◂ **17** south. Nessie T-shirts and all kinds of monster bric-à-brac are on sale. Excursion boats do regular monster-spotting

A round of golf in Inverness

cruises. You can cruise Loch Ness itself, and there are cruises from the Caledonian Canal into Loch Ness. Contact Jacobite Cruises, tel: 01463-233999; www.jacobite.co.uk.

Sonar and underwater cameras have been used by experts to close in on the mystery of the frequent Nessie sightings, and most involved seem to agree that not one, but several large aquatic creatures might roam the very murky depths of Loch Ness, surviving by eating eels and other fish.

Seven rivers feed this loch, bringing in millions of peat particles which reduce visibility to zero below 39ft (12m). At 23 miles (37km) long and about 1 mile (1.5 km) across, Loch Ness is generally about 699ft (213m) deep – though in one area the silted bottom is nearly 1,001ft (305m). That means enough space for a large family of the monster that has intrigued people ever since it was first reported in the 6th century – by no less revered a traveller than St Columba.

On the busy A82, after leaving the loch, it is virtually impossible to miss the dramatic ruins of **Urquhart Castle** (*see box on page 70*).

East of Inverness

About 5 miles (8km) east of Inverness is **Culloden Moor** (visitor centre open daily Apr–Oct 9am–6pm, Feb–Mar, Nov–Dec 10am–4pm; site open daily all year; charge; tel: 01463-790607), where Bonnie Prince Charlie's Highlanders and the Jacobite cause were defeated by 'Butcher' Cumberland's redcoats in 1746. Jacobite headstones, a visitor centre and museum, a 15-minute film and an information centre recall this last major battle fought on British soil. Near the battlefield is the impressive archaeological site of **Clava Cairns**. Three once-domed tombs are encircled by standing stones. To stand in a silent burial chamber dating back to 1800BC or 1500BC is a slightly eerie experience.

Between Inverness and Nairn is **Cawdor Castle** (May–early-Oct daily 10am–5.30pm; charge; www.cawdorcastle.com), a popular site set up to keep the visitor entertained. 'Three out of four Ghosts prefer Cawdor Castle', proclaims the sign at the castle's authentic drawbridge entrance. This fortress home of the Earls of Cawdor is the setting Shakespeare used for the murder of Duncan by Macbeth, although it was actually constructed two centuries after Macbeth's time. The castle has all the features to make it a romantic focus: a drawbridge, an ancient tower and fortified walls. The 1454 tower's Thorn Tree Room is a stone vault enclosing a 600-year-old hawthorn tree. The castle grounds have outstanding flower and kitchen gardens, a nature trail, and even a pitch-and-putt course. When you've seen the castle, head for nearby Cawdor village, with its delightful stone cottages set in beautifully tended gardens.

The impressive Clava Cairns

At Carrbridge the **Landmark Forest Adventure Park** (www.landmarkpark.co.uk) provides a wide range of outdoor activities for all the family.

Set against the spectacular backdrop of the Cairngorm Mountains, **Aviemore** *(see page 92)* is one of the most elaborate holiday centres in Scotland, its facilities open all winter for skiing. On a clear day, take a ride up into the mountains on the Cairngorm Mountain Railway. In 2003, the Cairngorms became a National Park, one of only two in Scotland – the other being Loch Lomond and the Trossachs *(see page 56)*.

Some 7 miles (11km) south, the excellent **Highland Wildlife Park** (www.highlandwildlifepark.org) at Kincraig has a drive-through area (if animals approach, close the windows and remain in your car). You should see the following animals: red deer, Highland cattle, ibex, Przewalski's wild horses, soay sheep, European bison and mouflon (forebears

Glen Coe offers great hiking

of domestic sheep). Stars of the walk-through section include arctic foxes, bears, and wildcats.

Ben Nevis and Glen Coe

The **Great Glen**, which follows the path of a geological fault, makes a scenic drive from Inverness south to Fort William. Near Fort William rises **Ben Nevis**, Great Britain's highest mountain, at 4,406ft (1,344m). More often than not, clouds obscure its rounded summit. The best view of the mountain is from the north, but it is most easily climbed from the west, starting near the bustling Highland touring centre of Fort William. Caution is advised here, as bad weather closes in quickly at the top of Ben Nevis and you can easily get lost.

19▶ From Loch Leven, historic **Glen Coe** cuts east through an impressive mountain range. Geology, flora, and fauna are illustrated at a visitor centre (Mar–Oct daily 10am–5pm, Nov–Feb Thur–Sun 10am–4pm; charge) operated by the National Trust. In the steep valley, you'll find a memorial to the 1692 massacre of the MacDonalds by the Campbell clan.

From Glen Coe and Fort William, you can take the famed **'Road to the Isles'**, with thoughts of Bonnie Prince Charlie in mind. The route goes past **Neptune's Staircase**, a series of eight lochs, designed by Thomas Telford as part of the Caledonian Canal. The road turns west to **Glenfinnan** (site of a memorial to fallen clansmen at the Battle of Culloden; *see page 22*) and north along the coast to **Morar**, with its white sandy beaches. One of Scotland's deepest lochs, Loch Morar, like Loch Ness, has its own monster, Morag. The end of the road is **Mallaig**, a little town with a picturesque harbour, where the ferry departs for Skye and other Hebridean islands.

The Northwest Coast

Near Dornie on the road towards Kyle of Lochalsh is the romantic and much-photographed **Eilean Donan Castle** (Mar–Oct daily 10am–6pm, opens 9am July–Aug; charge; www.eileandonancastle.com), connected to the land by a causeway. A Jacobite stronghold, it was destroyed by British warships, but was rebuilt in the 19th century. Today it is a popular tourist destination and has often been used as a film set; *Highlander* was filmed here. It contains a number of Jacobite relics.

West from Inverness towards the coast, the dramatic Loch Torridon area is well known for its mountains of red-brown sandstone and white quartzite. These are some of the world's oldest mountains, probably 600 million years old. The **Torridon Countryside Centre** in Torridon (Apr–Sept daily 10am–5pm; charge) offers guided walks in season.

The Gulf Stream works its magic at **Inverewe Garden** (gardens open daily all year 9.30am–4pm, extended hours in summer, visitor centre

A polar bear at the Highland Wildlife Park

Subtropical Inverewe Garden

Apr, Sept daily 10am–5pm, May–Aug 10am–6pm, Oct 10am–4pm; charge; tel: 0844-493 2227), a subtropical oasis overlooking Loch Ewe, on the same latitude as Juneau, Alaska. The garden was started in 1862 by 20-year-old Osgood Mackenzie on 12,000 acres (4,860 hectares) of barren land, and is one of the world's great plant collections. Late spring and early summer are the best seasons to visit; highlights include giant magnolias and the exotic Himalayan Hound's Tooth.

If you have time for a leisurely tour of Scotland's most spectacular scenery, turn north towards Ullapool. At a fine wooded spot just a minute's walk off the road below Loch Broom are the spectacular Falls of Measach, plunging 200ft (61m) into the **Corrieshalloch Gorge**.

22 Some of Scotland's most memorable scenery is along the jagged northwest coast above **Ullapool**, a fishing port and the ferry terminal for the Outer Hebrides. The secondary roads closest to the shore wind through beautiful country filled with mossy rocks, ferns, and hundreds of tiny lochans (small inland lochs). The first section goes through the **Inverpolly National Nature Reserve**. Near Lochinvar, strange stories gather around Suilven, the mount looming over the wild landscape (why don't animals graze on its slopes?). During the summer an excursion boat sets out from tiny Tarbet to **Handa Island**, a teeming bird sanctuary with huge sandstone cliffs and sandy beaches.

Along Scotland's northern coast near Durness is **Smoo Cave**, which can be found in a beautiful setting at the end of a dramatic sea inlet. The 'gloophole' through the cathedral-like limestone roof of the large outer cavern gets its name from the noise made by air rushing up through it at high tide. Inside the second cave is a 79-ft (24-m) waterfall. Short boat trips into the cave are available in summer.

A lighthouse with stout red foghorns stands on **Dunnet Head**, a windy promontory on the northernmost point of the Scottish mainland, overlooking a forbidding sea. If there's no mist, Orkney is visible on the horizon. Nearby **John o'Groats** is far better known, although it isn't quite the most northerly tip of Great Britain. The sign here declares it is 874 miles (1,406km) to Land's End in Cornwall, the greatest overland distance between any two points in Britain. From John o'Groats, you can take a ferry

Ullapool, one of the prettiest villages on the west coast

The Stacks of Duncansby

(May–Sept) to the **Orkney Islands**, which have fascinating archaeological remains – including the Neolithic village of Skara Brae and the Ring of Brodgar.

Offshore from **Duncansby Head**, with its clifftop lighthouse, are the unusual pillar-like Stacks of Duncansby. Inland and to the south, make a short detour from the angling centre of **Lairg** to the Falls of Shin where, with luck, you will see sizeable salmon leaping up low, churning falls along the river.

THE INNER HEBRIDES

Mull

Peaceful moorland glens, sombre mountains, appealing shorelines and one of Scotland's prettiest ports are among the attractions of the large western island of **Mull**. From **Oban**, the regular ferry takes 45 minutes to Craignure on Mull, and there is also a 15-minute ferry link between Fishnish Point and Lochaline across the Sound of Mull. In the summer, excursions go from Mull to several smaller islands.

Tobermory (pop. 700), the island's delightful little capital, fits snugly in a harbour ringed by forested hills and protected by flat, green Calve Island. Regattas are held here and golfers enjoy a splendid seascape from the links just above Tobermory. In 1588 a gold-laden galleon from the Spanish Armada sank here, but salvage efforts ever since have failed. Calgary, to the southwest, which has probably the best of

Mull's sandy beaches, inspired the name of the Canadian city about a century ago.

If you're driving and not in a rush, take the coastal road bordering Loch Na Keal. It's slow-going but scenic, along a single track beneath lonely cliffs and hills that are mauve with heather. Dozy sheep get out of your way reluctantly. Gaelic is still spoken here, particularly by the older generation. At the eastern point, visible from the Oban ferry, stand Mull's two castles, both open to the public.

Duart Castle (Apr Sun–Thur 11am–4pm, May–mid-Oct daily 10.30am–5.30pm; tea-room and shop open same hours; charge; www.duart castle.com), on its promontory, guards the Sound of Mull. Dating back to the 12th century, Duart Castle is the home of the chiefs of clan Maclean. The Maclean clan were once a formidable sea power.

An early evening boat trip in Oban

Torosay Castle (Easter–Oct daily 10.30am– 5pm; gardens open 9am–sunset; charge; www.torosay.com) is a Victorian family home and working farm. The gardens here are lined with statues and include woodland, Alpine and Japanese gardens as well as a walled garden. The castle can be reached by taking the narrow-gauge railway, which runs from Craignure to Torosay.

Iona

25 ▶ The sacred island of **Iona** lies just off the southwestern tip of Mull. St Columba and about a dozen followers came from Ireland to Iona in 563, bringing to Scotland the culture and learning of the Celtic church, which spread through all of Europe *(see page 14)*. Some 60 Scottish, Irish, French and Norwegian kings are buried on this sacred island. Centuries of onslaughts by Vikings and others have left no trace of the earliest communities.

Iona is reached via a one-track road and a ten-minute passenger ferry. Iona's 15th-century abbey has been reconstructed and restored. While the ideals of the abbey

St Martin's Cross on Iona

community cannot be faulted, modernism introduces a jarring note. Other sights are St Martin's Cross, carved in the 10th century; a small Norman chapel, built probably in 1072 by Queen Margaret; the attractive ruins of a 13th-century nunnery; and *Reilig Odhrain*, the graveyard where royalty, Highland chiefs, and more recent islanders are buried. Most of the older stones have been moved inside to preserve them from weather.

On a fine day, take a walk from here to North End where there are beaches of sparkling sand. Most of Iona's inhabitants (less than 100) live in the stone houses by the ferry landing. Sheep, cattle and a few fishing boats indicate occupations, but in the summer most islanders are involved with the throngs of visitors and pilgrims that arrive each year. From Iona you can take a boat trip to nearby **Staffa** island, which is home of the dramatic **Fingal's Cave**, a natural wonder which inspired part of Mendelssohn's *Hebrides Overture*. You can also get to Staffa from Mull or Oban.

> **Johnson's verdict**
>
> When he visited Iona in the year 1773, Samuel Johnson wrote: 'That man is little to be envied whose patriotism would not gain force upon the plain of Marathon, or whose piety would not grow warmer among the ruins of Iona'.

Skye

This best-loved Highland island is outrageously beautiful – whether the sun is shining or mists are swirling around its startling hills and idyllic glens. **Skye** is a 5-minute ferry trip from Kyle of Lochalsh, or 30 minutes from Mallaig. A bridge now links Kyleakin on Skye with Kyle of Lochalsh. **Portree**, ◄ 26 with its colourful harbour, is the island's main town. Together with **Broadford**, these are the most popular centres for touring, but the island has many quieter places to stay.

The interesting **Clan Donald Centre** and the beautiful **Armadale Castle Gardens** (daily Apr–Oct 9.30am– ◄ 27 5.30pm; charge; www.clandonald.com) are 16 miles (25km) south of Broadford, near the ferry terminal from Mallaig. For centuries the Macdonalds had styled themselves 'Lords of the Isles' and the museum has an exhibit detailing the history of the Highlands. The gardens and nature walks are outstanding.

Two remarkable ranges of peaks, the Black Cuillins in the south and the Quiraing in the north, make the island a hiker's

Cuillin Hills viewed from Kyle of Lochalsh

or rock-climber's paradise *(see page 91)*. Inside the wild and jagged **Cuillin Hills** is Loch Coruisk, which can be reached by boat from Elgol. Isolated by high peaks all around, the blue-black water of Coruisk has an eerie beauty. The hamlets of Ord and Tarskavaig are worth visiting on a clear day for their splendid views of the Cuillins.

Dunvegan Castle (daily Apr–Oct 10am–5.30pm, Nov–Mar group appointments only; charge; tel: 01470-521206; www.dunvegancastle.com), northwest of Portree, has been the stronghold of the chiefs of MacLeod for more than seven centuries and is still the home of the chief of the clan. On display within this sturdy loch-side fortress is the Fairy Flag, a fragile remnant of silk believed to have been woven in Rhodes during the 7th century. Supposedly it saved the MacLeods in clan battles twice, and still has the power to do so one more time. Rather more down-to-earth is a pit dungeon – 13ft (4m) deep – into which prisoners were lowered from an upstairs chamber, though the grim aspect of the dungeon is somewhat diluted by a 'prisoner' and an audio of his groans. Samuel Johnson and James Boswell were entertained here in 1773, and supplied with fresh horses to continue their journey.

From Dunvegan pier small boats make frequent half-hour trips to offshore rocks and islets to get close to the seals. The seals also appear, though less regularly, all around Skye's 998 miles (1,609km) of coastline.

The dramatic collection of rocks known as the **Quiraing**, accessed more easily than the Cuillins, dominates the landscape north of the secondary road between Staffin and Uig, the ferry port for the Outer Hebrides. Reached by foot, the various rock features here include the castellated crags of the Prison, the slender 100-ft (30-m) Needle and the Table, a meadow as large as a football field.

Far north at Kilmuir are the grave and monument to Skye's romantic heroine, **Flora MacDonald**, who smuggled fugitive Bonnie Prince Charlie, disguised as her female servant, to safety. On the picturesque coast of Staffin, the Kilt Rock is a curiously fluted cliff with a waterfall that plunges down to the sea. Be extremely careful on this lofty ridge.

A mile futher on, the Lealt Falls tumble down a long and accessible ravine into the sea at a pretty little cove. Salmon can sometimes be seen leaping here. Closer to Portree you will see a giant rock pinnacle called **Old Man of Storr**; there is a forest walk in the vicinity.

Old Man of Storr

WHAT TO DO

Wherever you might be staying in Scotland, particularly from spring to autumn, there's plenty to do. There's a range of information on the VisitScotland website (www.visitscotland.com) and various booklets can be ordered *(see page 131)*. The outdoors always beckons and you'll come across many local happenings as you travel around.

ENTERTAINMENT

Most newsagents in Glasgow and Edinburgh stock *The List*, which is a bi-weekly guide to events, theatre, cinema and clubs in both cities and their surrounding areas.

Special Events

Highland Games are staged all over the country during the summer months. In addition to kilted titans tossing a huge pine trunk – the famous caber – there'll be pipe and drum bands and accomplished shows of Highland dancing. The most famous of these events is the **Braemar Highland Gathering**, in early September, often attended by members of the royal family and the queen herself, a custom started by Queen Victoria. Also of interest are the agricultural shows and sheepdog trials held in a number of farming areas.

Throughout the summer there are country fairs and many re-enactments of battles and other historic events. In July, the **Scottish Transport Extravaganza** at Glamis Castle, an exhibition of vintage vehicles, is the largest event of its kind in Scotland. **Ceilidhs**, or **folk nights**, which are held frequently in all parts of Scotland, feature dancers, pipers, fiddlers and a range

Throwing the hammer at the Perth Highland Games

of other artists. Folk festivals are staged in centres like Wick and Inverness. There has been a revival of Gaelic music and both the traditional and the modern-style music performed by groups like Capercaillie and Runrig are enormously popular.

Of course, the most significant special event is the **Edinburgh International Festival**, which takes place in August *(see pages 29 and 97)*. Virtuoso performances of music, opera, dance, and theatre are staged by artists of international reputation. Tickets are in great demand so book early both for tickets and hotel rooms. The **Edinburgh Festival Fringe** is less predictable but increasingly popular and often highly innovative. Other cultural high spots include Glasgow's **West End Festival** and the **Perth Arts Festival**.

Performing on the Royal Mile during the Edinburgh Festival

Music and Theatre

The Theatre Royal in Glasgow is home to the **Scottish Opera**. The Glasgow Royal Concert Hall is the main venue for classical music, with regular concerts by the **Royal Scottish National Orchestra**. Both also perform regularly in Edinburgh, home to the prestigious Scottish Chamber Orchestra. The churches in both cities regularly host excellent concerts. The prestigious BBC Scottish Symphony Orchestra is based at City Halls in Glasgow, taking live music across the country.

Both cities have first-rate **theatre** scenes, with high-quality productions all year round. The Citizens' Theatre in Glasgow presents serious drama, with more avant-garde shows at the Tramway and the Tron. In Edinburgh, the Traverse launches experimental work and the Royal Lyceum mounts a classical repertory. Shows, musicals and touring companies are also on the agenda. An important theatre season takes place over the summer in **Pitlochry** *(see page 63)*. Other centres for regional theatre are St Andrews, Banchory, and Tobermory and Dervaig on Mull. Stirling's Tolbooth is a centre for the arts and music, and a Robert Burns festival takes place in Dumfries.

Major **rock bands** appear at Hampden Park in Glasgow or occasionally Murrayfield Stadium in Edinburgh. Other main venues in Glasgow are the SECC and the Barrowlands. The **Glasgow International Jazz Festival** in June brings in jazz musicians from all over the world.

Festival fever

Also held during the Edinburgh Festival are the Military Tattoo, Book Festival, Film Festival and the Jazz and Blues Festival. For details visit www.edinburgh festivals.co.uk.

Clubs and Pubs

Pubs are very popular with the locals everywhere in Scotland and are especially crowded around the end of the working day and at weekends. The scene is lively and while the drinking man's bar still exists, most pubs now have a relaxed and friendly atmosphere. Thanks to changes in Scottish licensing laws, even children are welcome in many pubs. An increasing number serve good food. Many pubs in the cities also offer live music in the evening. Some pubs, especially in Edinburgh, have their own resident folk or jazz musicians. In Glasgow, you can choose between traditional pubs and upmarket, fashionable bars. Café-bars are plentiful in Edinburgh.

Fly fishing

SPORT AND RECREATION

Scotland's outdoors attracts more visitors than its castles, museums or even the Edinburgh Festival.

Fishing

Scotland's rivers, lochs and coastal waters offer some of the finest game fishing in Europe. Much of it is free or very cheap; you don't need a general fishing licence, just a local permit. However, casting your line in the highly prized salmon beats costs hundreds of pounds per week, and you may have to book a year ahead for the privilege.

The **Spey, Tay** and **Tweed** are famous for salmon, sea trout and brown trout, though these fish also run in other Scottish waters. Most angling is fly; occasionally spinner or bait is permitted. If you'd like to learn the difference between a dry fly and an insect or how to stay upright while wading and casting in a rushing burn, experts are on hand all over Scotland. Contact VisitScotland (www.fishpal.com/visit scotland or *see page 131*) for information on fishing, which give details of the best places, seasons and necessary permits. Fishing for salmon and sea trout is not allowed on Sundays and it is now illegal for anglers to sell rod-caught salmon. Coarse fishing for perch and pike is permitted year-round, including Sundays, and can be very good, particularly in southern waters.

Sea-angling trips run from ports along the Scottish coast and the islands; or you can fish from countless perches on the shoreline. Some species of fish, such as dogfish and mackerel, can be found in abundance, and towards the end of the summer you might well hook blue or porbeagle shark.

For more information, contact the **Scottish Anglers National Association**, National Game Angling Centre, The Pier, Loch Leven, Kinross; tel: 01577-861116; www.sana. org.uk.

Golf

Scotland is the original home of golf, a powerful lure for visitors wanting to play on the famous links. Many of Scotland's courses are municipal courses open to everyone. To play the famous courses, it helps to have a letter from your golf club at home stating your experience and handicap. If you choose your hotels or a special golfing-holiday package with care, you can play a different course each day for a week. The Scots make a distinction between two types of courses: links courses are on or near the sea; parkland (or heathland) courses are inland, often on hilly terrain.

St Andrews, home of the **Royal and Ancient Golf Club** has six courses of its own (a seventh is being constructed), plus 12 more within easy reach in northeast Fife. Visitors with ambi-

Links Lineage

When exactly golf began along the sandy coast in this chilly and windy land isn't clear, but the earliest record dates from 1457, when James II tried to outlaw golf as a menace to national security – too many Scots marksmen were skipping archery practice to swing at the little ball. Mary, Queen of Scots loved the game so much that she risked criticism by taking to the fairways while in mourning for her murdered husband. She is thought to have played at Bruntsfield in Edinburgh, probably the oldest course on which golf is still played today.

tion to play the historic **Old Course** should apply in writing to the St Andrews Links Trust, www.standrews.org.uk, in September for the following year for a pre-booked tee-time, or enter the daily 'ballot', a lottery to determine which lucky applicants will fill vacancies and cancellations the following day. You can book any of the St Andrews courses at the **Club**, tel: 01334-466666. Other outstanding Scottish golf courses include **Carnoustie**, **Royal Troon**, **Gleneagles**, **Muirfield**, **Royal Dornoch** and **Turnberry**.

Biking, Hiking and Mountain-Climbing

Biking. For more information about bicycling in Scotland see the VisitScotland website: http://cycling.visitscotland. com. The rolling hills of **Fife** are especially good for cycling and there is a 300-mile (500-km) sign posted cycle network. Contact them on the web: www.fife-cycle-ways.co.uk.

Biking in the Cairngorms

Hiking. Scotland's beautiful landscape offers unrivalled opportunities for hiking and hill walking. The West Highland Way begins in Milngavie north of Glasgow and continues on past Loch Lomond up to Fort William. The Southern Upland Way and Speyside Way are also popular for long-distance walks. There are also many guided walks. In the Highlands, particularly, you will find nature walks and hill or plateau excursions led by trained naturalists. Week-long hikes over moors and glens include meals and accommodation in the price. At **Glen Coe** and **Torridon** the National Trust for Scotland conducts several superb guided walks. VisitScotland have an excellent walking guide (http://walking. visitscotland.com).

Mountain-climbing. You can take a strenuous walk up Britain's highest mountain, **Ben Nevis** *(see page 74)*, climb the peaked ridges of the Isle of **Arran** *(see page 48)* or go rock climbing in the Black Cuillins, depending on your skills. While their height is not great, the remote **Cuillins** on Skye offer some of the most challenging climbing in Britain *(see page 82)*. The **Mountaineering Council of Scotland** in Perth, tel: 01738-493942, can provide maps and telephone numbers to call for advice.

> ### Climbing caveats
>
> Despite a concentrated campaign for safety, mountain climbers continue to get into trouble in Scotland. Always get local advice on weather and conditions. Weather can change rapidly and suddenly, especially in the Highlands. Be sure you take the proper equipment and let someone know where you are going. Never go alone.

Boating and Watersports

Depending on your expertise, you can hire any sort of boat to explore Scotland's marvellous inland and coastal waters. **Sailing** schools offer courses for beginners all along Scotland's coast. If you have documentation to prove your proficiency, you may be able to charter larger craft without a skipper.

Water-skiing is popular on the placid waters of Scotland's lochs. **Windsurfing** is available at all levels inland, on lochs, or on the open sea. Summer days can be surprisingly hot, and swimming opportunities are abundant. Be alert, however, for dangerous undertows and rip currents off western coasts.

Football is hugely popular

The transparency of Scotland's waters makes them ideal for **scuba diving**. There are sub-aqua sites all around the coast, in various inland lochs and on the islands.

For further information on watersports in Scotland contact VisitScotland's website http://adventure.visit scotland.com).

Pony Trekking and Riding

All over Scotland there are horse and pony centres where you can ride by the hour, half day or full day. Pony treks are led by expert guides and some are suitable for young children. The **Scottish Equestrian Association** represents all equestrian interests in Scotland and provides a database of resources; www.s-e-a.org.uk. Horseback trail riding is only for experienced riders. Some centres offer accommodation and weekly programmes with a different excursion each day.

Skiing

Scotland has five major downhill ski centres: **Cairngorm** in Inverness-shire, **White Corries** in Glen Coe, the **Nevis mountain range** in Inverness-shire, the **Lecht** and **Glenshee**, both in Aberdeenshire. The Cairngorms are Britain's highest mountains, and **Aviemore**, its centre, has buses to the ski areas, which have runs for skiers of all abilities. You'll find instructors, chairlifts, equipment hire, tows and accommodation at all the main ski areas; there's also the Cairngorm Mountain Railway. The ski season is December to May, though snowfall can be unpredictable (for updates: http://ski.visitscotland.com).

Spectator Sports

Rugby and football are as popular in Scotland as in the rest of the UK. Glasgow's Celtic and Rangers are the most successful soccer teams. International competitions take place in Hampden Park Stadium. You may also want to observe the Scottish game of curling, a bit like bowling on ice, which has been practised in Scotland for at least 400 years.

SHOPPING

Shops are generally open 9am–5.30pm Monday to Saturday (a few places may close on Saturday afternoon), and major shopping centres in cities are also open on Sunday. In the Highlands, however, Sunday closing is the rule. In smaller towns, check whether there is an early closing day.

Princes Square shopping centre in Glasgow

Glasgow is Scotland's major shopping city. Main areas are the smart, upmarket **Princes Square**, the newer **Buchanan Galleries** and **Buchanan Street**. Also popular is the St Enoch Centre, the largest glass structure in Europe. In Edinburgh the main shopping is on **Princes Street**, with fashion chains, bookshops and department stores. For gifts, tartans and other Scottish wares, there are plenty of shops on the **Royal Mile**. For upmarket shopping, visit Multrees Walk just off St Andrew Square, centred around the Harvey Nichols store.

Value Added Tax (VAT). Almost all merchandise and services are subject to 20 percent Value Added Tax (VAT). For major purchases over a certain amount of money, overseas visitors can get a VAT refund. Note that this applies only to shops that are members of the Retail Export Scheme. When you make your purchase, request a signed form and a stamped pre-addressed envelope; have your form stamped by British Customs as you leave the country and post the form back to the shop to obtain a refund. You can also avoid the VAT if you do your shopping in duty-free shops – look for the sign.

Colourful shops along West Bow in Edinburgh

Visitors from EU countries should present the form to their home customs, who will insert the local VAT rate for the goods. This form should also be posted back to the shop for a refund.

What to Buy

Art and Antiques. The Scottish art scene is an active one. Look for prints and affordable works by young Scottish artists. Victorian antiques and old prints and maps are also a good buy.

Crafts. In the Highlands you will find interesting stoneware and salt-glazed pottery. There are potters, jewellery makers and other craftspeople on the Isles of Mull and Skye. Unusual 'heathergems' jewellery is made from stems of heather. Look out for wood and stag-horn carvings, Celtic designs, handknits and hand-made greetings cards.

Crystal. A number of high-quality glass and crystal producers have come from Scotland, including Caithness Glass, Selkirk Glass, Edinburgh Crystal and Stuart Crystal. There's also the

Dog and whisky in Edinburgh

Caithness Glass visitor centre in Crieff (tel: 01764-654014), where you can buy beautiful paperweights.

Kilts and Tartans. A number of shops in Edinburgh, Glasgow, Stirling and Aberdeen specialise in made-to-measure kilts, or full Highland dress. These shops will be glad to help you find your family tartan.

Knitwear and Woollens. Scottish knitwear includes cashmere pullovers and cardigans and Shetland and Fair Isle sweaters. Tartan woollens can be bought by the yard, and you can see them woven at several woollen mills. Harris tweed and sheepskin rugs are also popular buys.

Jewellery. In Glasgow (and elsewhere), look for sterling and enamel jewellery made from the designs of Charles Rennie Mackintosh. Silvercraft from Orkney and Shetland has designs inspired by Norse mythology. Celtic-designed jewellery, clan brooches and ornate kilt pins are often produced in pewter. And for the romantics there's the delicately worked luckenbooth, a traditional Scottish love token.

Whisky. Scotch whisky is not less expensive in Scotland, but you'll find brands that you never knew existed, so take the opportunity to discover an unusual malt.

CHILDREN'S ACTIVITIES

VisitScotland's website http://families.visitscotland.com gives information on where to take the kids. Children enjoy exploring Scottish castles and there are many country parks with farm animals and playgrounds. Highland Games offer colourful spectacles with plenty of side shows *(see page 85)*.

In Edinburgh, children will enjoy the Museum of Childhood on the Royal Mile *(see page 34)* and the National Museum of Scotland *(see page 33)*. Older children will like the scary thrills of the **Edinburgh Dungeon**, 31 Market Street, next to Waverley Bridge (open daily 10am–5pm, until 7pm end June to end Aug; admission fee; tel: 0131-2401001). Both children and adults will find Our Dynamic Earth *(see page 36)* fascinating. **Edinburgh Zoo**, 134 Corstorphine Road, 3 miles (5km) from the centre, is Scotland's largest, on 80 acres (32 hectares) of hillside parkland (open daily Mar and Oct 9am–5pm, Apr–Sept 9am–6pm, Nov–Feb 9am–4.30pm; admission fee; penguin parade 2.15pm 21 Apr– 30 Sept; tel: 0131-334 9171; www.edinburghzoo.org.uk).

Scotland is full of child-friendly attractions

At Coatbridge on the M8 motorway near Glasgow, the **Time Capsule** (www.thetimecapsule.info) puts on amusements including ice-skating with a woolly mammoth.

Calendar of Events

January Celtic Connections, traditional music festival, www.celtic connections.com, Glasgow. 25 January: Burns Night, Scotland-wide. Last Tuesday in January: Up Helly Aa, fire festival, Lerwick, Shetland.

February Fort William Mountain Film Festival, for outdoor enthusiasts, www.mountainfilmfestival,co.uk.

March Glasgow International Comedy Festival, www.glasgowcomedy festival.com. Easter events at Scotland's ski resorts, www.ski-scotland.com.

April Edinburgh International Harp Festival, www.harpfestival.co.uk. Scottish Grand National, Ayr, www.ayr-racecourse.co.uk.

Late April–May Perth Festival of the Arts, www.perthfestival.co.uk. Spirit of Speyside Whisky Festival, Moray & Speyside www.spiritofspeyside.com.

June Common Ridings, festival of marking town boundaries on horseback, Scottish Borders. West End Festival, including the Midsummer Carnival, Glasgow, www.westendfestival.co.uk. Scottish Traditional Boat Festival, Portsoy, Aberdeenshire, www. scottishtraditionalboatfestival. org.uk. Royal Highland Show, farming event, Ingliston, near Edinburgh, www.royalhighland show.org. Edinburgh International Film Festival, www.edfilmfest.org.uk.

July Barclays Scottish Open, golf tournament, Loch Lomond, www.barclays scottishopen.co.uk. The Wickerman Festival, alternative music festival, East Kirkcarswell, Dumfries & Galloway, www.the wickermanfestival.co.uk. Edinburgh Jazz and Blues Festival. Glasgow International Jazz Festival.

August Edinburgh International Festival, www.eif.co.uk. Edinburgh Fringe Festival, www.edfringe.com. Edinburgh Military Tattoo, www. edintattoo. co,uk. World Pipe Band Championship, with over 200 bands, Glasgow.

September First Saturday: Braemar Highland Gathering, www.braemar gathering.org. Doors Open Days, visit the country's best architecture for free, Scotland-wide, www.doorsopendays.org.uk.

October Royal National Mod, Gaelic language festival, different locations.

November 30 November (and week running up to it), St Andrew's Day, St Andrews and Scotland-wide.

December 31 December: Hogmanay, Scotland-wide. Stonehaven Fireball Festival, traditional parade, www.stonehavenfireballs.co.uk.

EATING OUT

Not the least of Scotland's many surprises is the amount of good cooking to be found, even in remote spots. Scottish chefs have in recent years won accolades at international culinary competitions, and the better hotels and country house hotels may be staffed by award-winning chefs. The tourist office's 'Taste of Scotland' initiative has encouraged chefs to rethink traditional dishes, using the freshest local ingredients. Chefs make full use of these local basics: fresh salmon and trout, herring, beef, venison, grouse, pheasant, potatoes, raspberries, and other fruit and vegetables. Oatmeal turns up in all kinds of dishes. Long gone are the days of Samuel Johnson's oft-quoted remark about oats after he toured the northern regions of Scotland: '...a grain which in England is generally given to horses, but in Scotland supports the people'.

A full Scottish breakfast

Much Scottish fare is hearty, intended to act as a fortification against the weather. Whenever possible, try traditional dishes, which are often delicious. Vegetarian options are widely available in the cities, and are increasingly offered in smaller towns and villages.

WHEN TO EAT

Outside the cities, restaurants, roadside inns and snack bars are rather thin on the ground. Even in the cities, many of the finest Scottish restaurants are in hotels; non-residents are

Further info

The List's Eating and Drinking Guide provides listings for Edinburgh and Glasgow; www.list.co.uk. For restaurants serving traditional Scottish food visit www.taste-of-scotland.com.

usually welcome, but check with guest houses or smaller establishments. In the summer, it is a good idea to book ahead, particularly if the restaurant is known for its fine cuisine. If you are touring, picnic lunches are a good idea – you may find yourself miles from any food outlets and there is certainly no shortage of lovely sites.

Breakfast, usually from around 8am–10am, is provided by practically every hotel and guest house in Scotland. Away from major centres, restaurants may not serve lunch before noon or much after 2pm, and dinner may only be served between 7 and 9pm.

In general, restaurant prices compare favourably with those south of the border. This does not prevent certain Scottish establishments – proud of their accolades and perhaps conscious of the shortness of the 'season' – from charging prices that would not be out of place in London's West End. Keep in mind the inclusion in restaurant prices of 20 percent VAT sales tax, and often a 10 percent service charge. A full Scottish breakfast is usually included in your hotel or bed and breakfast tariff.

While a light lunch at midday and more substantial dinner in the evening may be the style in tourist areas, conversely, in the countryside dinner is sometimes what the substantial midday meal is called, while the lighter evening meal may be called tea or supper.

WHAT TO EAT

Breakfast

Unlike England, where some hotels have converted to the 'continental breakfast', the Scottish breakfast still gives you the works. Porridge is served with cream or milk (and sugar, though this is frowned upon by traditionalists, who prefer salt and use water instead of milk), followed by fruit juice, fresh fruit, eggs, sausage, bacon, tomatoes, mushrooms, potato scones, rolls, jam and marmalade. A special touch is the addition of the Scottish kipper and smoked haddock – it's hard to argue with the conventional wisdom that Loch Fyne kippers are best, but it is equally hard to find a smoked herring from anywhere in Scotland that isn't delicious. The famous Arbroath smokies are salted haddock flavoured with hot birch or oak smoke. Finnan haddock (or haddie) are salted and smoked over peat. Pâtés of kipper, trout, smoked salmon and haddock have become favourite starters in good restaurants.

Scotch Broth

Traditional Scottish soups are best if they are homemade. Try a few of the following:

Cock-a-leekie – a seasoned broth made from boiling fowl with leeks and at times onions and prunes. Consumed for at least 400 years and dubbed the national soup of Scotland.

Partan bree – creamed crab (partan) soup.

Scotch broth – a variety of vegetables in a barley-thickened soup with mutton or beef.

Cullen skink – milky broth of Finnan haddock with onions and potatoes.

Lorraine – a creamy chicken soup made with nutmeg, almonds and lemon, named after Mary of Guise-Lorraine.

Oatmeal – made with onion, leek, carrot and turnip.

Try Arbroath smokies while in Scotland

Main Courses

Fish and Shellfish. Scottish smoked salmon is famous all over the world, thanks to the special flavours introduced by the distinctive peat or oak-chip smoking process. Farmed salmon is now widely available, and while the purist may argue that it isn't as good as the wild variety, there are few people who can actually tell the difference.

Nothing is better than a whole fresh salmon poached with wine and vegetables. The west coast is renowned for the excellence of its lobster, scallops, crayfish, mussels and oysters.

Meat and Game. Scottish beef rivals the best in Europe. Aberdeen Angus steak is a favourite, served with a mushroom-and-wine sauce. Whisky goes into many sauces served with beef: Gaelic steak, for instance, is seasoned with garlic and fried with sautéed onions, with whisky added during the cooking process. Whisky is also used in preparing seafood, poultry and game. *Forfar bridies* are pastry puffs stuffed with minced steak and onions. If you are lucky, you might also find beef collops (slices) in pickled walnut sauce. Veal is rather scarce. In recent years, lamb has appeared more frequently, sometimes in ingenious dishes.

Game still abounds in Scotland. After the shooting season opens (on the 'glorious 12th' of August), grouse is an expensive but much sought-after dish, served in a pie or roasted with crispy bacon and served with bread sauce or fried breadcrumbs. Venison appears frequently on the menu, often roasted or in a casserole. You will also find pheasant, guinea fowl, quail and hare in terrines, pâtés and game pies.

Haggis. Haggis, Scotland's national dish, hardly deserves its horrific reputation among non-Scots. Properly made, it consists of chopped-up sheep's innards, oatmeal, onions, beef suet and seasoning, boiled in a sewn-up sheep's stomach bag. Haggis is traditionally accompanied by *chappit tatties* and *bashed neeps* – mashed potatoes and turnips.

Haggis and whisky

Other traditional dishes are *Scotch eggs*: hard-boiled eggs coated with sausage meat and breadcrumbs, deep-fried and eaten hot or cold. *Scotch woodcock* is toast topped with anchovy and scrambled egg.

Potatoes and Oatmeal. Potatoes are a particular local pride. *Stovies* are leftovers from the Sunday roast, usually including potatoes, onions, carrots, gravy and occasionally the meat, cooked in the dripping. *Rumbledethumps* are a mixture of boiled cabbage and mashed potatoes (sometimes onions or chives and grated cheese are added).

Skirlie

Skirlie is a mixture of oatmeal and onions flavoured with thyme. Oatmeal also turns up as a coating on such foods as herring and cheese and in desserts *(see below)*.

You should not have to go all the way to northernmost Caithness for Scotland's basic dish of *tatties* (potatoes boiled in their skin) and herrings. And in the Orkney Islands they like *clapshot* (potatoes and turnips mashed together and seasoned with fresh black pepper) to accompany their haggis.

Afternoon Tea, Dessert and Cheese

Tea rooms all over Scotland offer afternoon tea, with sandwiches, cakes and other delicacies. Shortbread is, of course, a Scottish speciality. Another classic Scottish speciality is rich, dark Dundee cake, made with dried fruits and spices and topped with almonds. Dundee also contributed bitter orange marmalade to the world in the 1700s. Scones and bannocks (oatmeal cakes) are among the great array of Scottish baked and griddled goods. A teatime treat is Scotch pancakes, served with butter and marmalade or honey. Oatcakes come either rough or smooth and they are eaten on their own or with butter, pâté, jam, or crowdie, Scotland's centuries-old version of cottage cheese. In Edinburgh, the afternoon tea at the Balmoral Hotel is famous, and in Glasgow, don't miss going to one of the Willow Tea Rooms, designed by Charles Rennie Mackintosh.

For dessert, you'll see various combinations of cheese, with red berries or black cherries and vanilla ice cream. Cranachan, a tasty Scottish speciality, consists of toasted oatmeal and cream and whisky or rum topped with nuts and raspberries or other soft fruit. Rhubarb-and-ginger tart is worth looking out for, as is butterscotch tart.

Scotland produces several excellent varieties of cheddar cheese and recent years have seen a rediscovery of old Scottish cheeses. Produced (although on a small scale) throughout the country, the speciality cheeses are characterised by a high degree of individuality. Try Criffel, Lanark blue, Isle of Mull or creamy Crannog or Orkney Cheddar.

WHAT TO DRINK

A huge amount of folklore surrounds every aspect of **Scotch whisky**, from its distillation using pure mountain water, to the aroma of the peat, to its storage, all the way to the actual drinking. The word 'whisky' derives from the Gaelic *uisge beatha*

Glenfiddich Distillery

'water of life'. It is available in two basic types – *malt* (distilled solely from malted barley) and *grain* (made from malted barley and grain). Most of the Scotch sold today is blended, combining malt and grain whiskies. There are now more than 2,000 brands of authentic Scotch whisky.

The malt whiskies come primarily from Speyside and the Highlands, and each has

Whisky in Glen Coe

its own distinctive flavour: dry, smoky, peppery, peaty or sweet. Purists insist that a single-malt whisky should be drunk only neat or with plain water – never with other mixers, although these are acceptable with blended Scotch, even by Scots.

After dinner, Scotland's version of Irish coffee, which naturally uses local whisky, may be called a 'Gaelic coffee'. A rusty nail, believed for obvious reasons to have associations with a coffin nail, is one measure of malt whisky plus one measure of Drambuie. A 'Scotch mist' is made from whisky, squeezed lemon rind and crushed ice, shaken well. An 'Atholl Brose' blends oatmeal, heather honey and whisky.

Because of the country's long-standing association with France – the 'Auld Alliance' against the English – good French **wine**, especially claret, was on Scottish tables before it was widely available in England. Most reputable hotels and restaurants offer an extensive wine list, often now including good wines from New Zealand, Australia and Chile.

Scotland is proud of its **beer**. The Scottish equivalent of English 'bitter' is called 'heavy', and should be served at room temperature. The 'half and a half' featured in old-fashioned pubs is a dram of whisky with a half pint of beer as a chaser.

PLACES TO EAT

We have used the following symbols to give an idea of the price for a meal for one person without wine or service.

££££ over £40   **££** £18–£28
£££ £28–£40   **£** under £18

EDINBURGH AND LOTHIAN

Atrium ££–£££ *10 Cambridge Street, tel: 0131-228 8882, www.atriumrestaurant.co.uk.* Open Monday–Friday for lunch, Monday–Saturday for dinner. In an atmospheric setting, modern Scottish cuisine is offered, with local produce showcased in many of the dishes. A vegetarian alternative is always included. Great for dinner when going to nearby theatres; reservations recommended.

Champany Inn £££ *Champany, Linlithgow, West Lothian, tel: 01506-834532, www.champany.com.* Open Monday–Friday for lunch and dinner, Saturday dinner only. Acclaimed for its steaks and wine cellar, and set in an old mill with beamed ceilings and antique tables. An informal, moderately priced 'Chop and Ale House' adjoins. Reservations advised.

Creelers ££ *3 Hunter Square, tel: 0131-220 4447, www.creelers.co.uk.* Open daily for lunch and dinner. Much of the seafood produce comes from Arran where the owners have a smokehouse and another restaurant. There are game and vegetarian dishes, too.

Gurka Brigade £ *9a Antigua Street, tel: 0131-556 6446, www.gurkhabrigade.com.* Open daily for lunch and dinner. This restaurant serves fresh, delicious Nepalese cuisine, and gives a friendly welcome.

Henderson's of Edinburgh £–££ *94 Hanover Street, tel: 0131-225 2131, www.hendersonsofedinburgh.co.uk.* Open Monday–

Saturday for breakfast, lunch and dinner. Henderson's still has its salad bar basement restaurant but now has a bistro and deli too. Perfect for vegetarians, it offers salads, vegetarian pasta and moussaka, or vegetarian haggis with neeps and tatties. Good desserts, organic wines, plus live jazz and other music genres in the evening.

Howies £–££ *29 Waterloo Place, tel: 0131-556 5766, www. howies.uk.com.* Open daily for lunch and dinner. Informal restaurant serving food consisting of fresh, tasty ingredients in a pleasant atmosphere. Also open from 11am for coffee and pastries.

Iggs £££ *15 Jeffery Street, tel: 0131-557 8184, www.iggs.co. uk.* Open Monday–Saturday for lunch and dinner. Iggs is where Spanish cooking deftly uses Scottish produce and the result has justly received acclaim and awards. Just off the Royal Mile, reservations are recommended. Its tapas bar, Barioja, is at 19 Jeffrey Street.

Number One £££ *The Balmoral Hotel, 1 Princes Street tel: 0131-557 6727, www.restaurantnumberone.com.* Open daily for lunch and dinner. World-class cooking, using the best of Scottish produce, at this wonderfully stylish Michelin-starred restaurant.

Vin Caffè ££ *Multrees Walk, tel: 0131-557 0088, www. valvonacrolla.co.uk.* Open Monday–Saturday for coffee, lunch and dinner, Sunday lunch only. Part of the legendary Italian family institution, Valvona and Crolla, so well loved throughout the city, this first floor restaurant is superb.

Vintners Rooms £££–££££ *The Vaults, 87 Giles Street, Leith, tel: 0131-554 6767, www.vitnersrooms.com.* Open Tuesday–Saturday for lunch and dinner. This well-known restaurant is in an old wine warehouse. Come here for a slice of France in Leith, for traditional cooking with a contemporary twist. The wine list is impressive.

The Witchery by the Castle £££ *352 Castlehill, Royal Mile, tel: 0131-225 5613, www.thewitchery.com.* Open daily for lunch and dinner. Whether it is Aberdeen Angus beef or Scottish lobster the cooking at the Witchery won't disappoint and a galaxy of celebrities would agree. Special light lunch menus help to keep the cost down.

SOUTH AND BORDERS

Fouters £££ *2a Academy Street, Ayr, tel: 01292-261391, www.fouters.co.uk.* Open Tuesday–Saturday for lunch and dinner. Located in the cellars of an old bank, this informal restaurant offers hearty portions of fine Scottish produce prepared in a traditional, but subtle way. Try the special seafood night menu, featuring scallops, mussels and Arbroath smokies. Reservations recommended.

Kailzie Gardens Restaurant ££ *Near Peebles (on B7062), tel: 01721-722807, www.kailziegardens.com.* Open for coffee, lunch and tea. Under new management in 2010 this delightful restaurant serves home-cooked lunches and fine afternoon teas.

Marmions Brasserie ££ *Buccleuch Street, Melrose, the Borders, tel: 01896-82224, www.marmionbrasserie.co.uk.* Open Monday–Saturday for lunch and dinner. Relaxed, friendly restaurant with good use of local produce. A good place to stop for lunch when touring the Border abbeys.

Simply Scottish £–££ *High Street, Jedburgh, Roxburghshire, tel: 01835-864696.* Open daily for coffee, lunch and dinner. A restaurant and café, it serves sophisticated and contemporary Scottish cuisine, made from the freshest ingredients. Reservations suggested at dinner.

GLASGOW

Babbity Bowster £–££ *16–18 Blackfriars Street, tel: 0141-552 5055.* Open daily for lunch and dinner. The popular downstairs bar/restaurant serves seafood and Scottish fare, but for a quieter, more intimate dinner, it's advisable to eat upstairs in the charming dining room. You can stay here too, but it can sometimes be very noisy.

Café Gandolfi £ 64 Albion St, tel: 0141-552 6813. Open daily for morning coffee, lunch, tea and dinner. In the heart of Glasgow's merchant city, this restaurant offers good, simple food in a pleasant atmosphere. Another popular branch is at Habitat in the Buchanan Galleries.

Drum and Monkey £–££ 93–5 St Vincent Street, tel: 0141-221 6636. This casual bar-restaurant serves Scottish-French cuisine daily in Victorian surroundings and is a local favourite.

El Sabor £–££ 17 Bell Street, Merchant Square, tel: 0141-552 3400, www.elsabor.co.uk. Open daily for lunch and dinner. This restaurant has friendly staff who serve good Spanish cuisine, including excellent tapas.

Jamie's Italian ££ 1 George Square, tel: 0141-552 3400, www.jamieoliver.com/italian. Open daily for lunch and dinner. The latest of Jamie Oliver's Italian-style restaurants opened in 2010. Honest Italian rustic seasonal fare.

La Parmigiana ££ 447 Great Western Road, tel: 0141-334 0686, www.laparmigiana.co.uk. Open Monday– Saturday for lunch and dinner. This small, family-run establishment in Glasgow's west end serves Italian cuisine in elegant surroundings. The restaurant prides itself on the authenticity and excellence of its cuisine.

Rogano ££££ 11 Exchange Place, tel: 0141-248 4055, www.roganoglasgow.com. Open daily for lunch and dinner. Open since 1935, this famous restaurant has an Art-Dec interior. It specialises in the freshest of seafood and has an excellent wine list. Downstairs, Café Rogano is a more informal, moderately priced restaurant. Reservations essential.

Willow Tea Rooms £ *217 Sauchiehall Street, tel: 0141-332 052, www.willowtearooms.co.uk. 1.* Open Monday– Saturday for breakfast, lunch and tea; Sunday for lunch and tea only. Charles Rennie Mackintosh's original tearooms (upstairs from the jewellery shop on the ground floor). Mackintosh designed the details of the building's interior. Recreated Willow Tea Rooms are at 97 Buchanan Street. Both serve the sandwiches, cakes and tea you would expect.

Windows £££ *In the Carlton George, 44 West George Street, 7th floor, tel: 0141-354 5070, www.carlton.nl/george.* Open daily for lunch, pre-theatre meals and dinner. An excellent and attractive restaurant with interesting rooftop views. Only the freshest produce is used. It is advisable to book.

CENTRAL SCOTLAND

But 'n' Ben ££ *Auchmithie, tel: 01241-877223.* Open Wednesday–Monday for lunch, Monday and Wednesday– Saturday for dinner. This restaurant housed in a row of cottages is best-known for its high tea and inexpensive seafood dishes which are served in comfortable surroundings by friendly staff.

The Beautiful Mountain £ *11–13 Belmont Street, Aberdeen, tel: 01224-645353, www.thebeautifulmoutain.co.uk.* Open Monday–Saturday for breakfast, lunch and tea. One of the best cafés in Aberdeen with scrumptious cakes and light lunches.

The Cellar ££–££££ *24 East Green, Anstruther, Fife, tel: 01333-310378, www.thecellaranstruther.co.uk.* Easter–October open daily for lunch and dinner, November–Easter closed Sunday and Monday. This famed seafood restaurant located in the waterfront town of Anstruther has a menu that ranges from the renowned crayfish-and-mussel bisque to Scottish beef and lamb. Excellent wine list.

Clachan Inn £ *2 Main Street, Drymen, tel: 01360-660824, www.clachaninndrymen.co.uk.* Open daily for lunch and dinner. Very child-friendly, with special children's menu. Pub menu that includes fish and chips and hearty casseroles.

Green Inn £££ *9 Victoria Road, Ballater, tel: 01339-755701, www.green-inn.com.* Open for dinner: April–October Monday–Saturday; November–March Tuesday– Saturday. For an authentic Scottish dining experience, try this homely restaurant. Good wine list.

The Kilberry Inn ££–£££ *Kilberry Road, Kilberry, tel: 01880-770223, www.kilberryinn.com.* Open Tuesday–Saturday for lunch and dinner. It's worth seeking out this wonderful restaurant with rooms, reached by a single-track road between Tarbet and Lochgilphead. Scottish restaurant of the year in 2009, the local produce is used to wonderful effect.

Old Boatyard £-££ *Fishmarket Quay, Arbroath, tel: 01241-879995, www.oldboatyard.co.uk.* Open daily for lunch and tea. An attractive modern building, which retains a traditional feel, the restaurant is located in Arbroath's newly developed harbour. Seafood is a favourite, but there are plenty of other tasty choices.

Peat Inn ££–££££ *By Cupar, Fife, tel: 01334-840206, www. thepeatinn.co.uk.* Open Tuesday–Saturday for lunch and dinner. A pioneer in the revival of Scottish cuisine, this restaurant is a dining experience. Reservations recommended. If you want to stay here as well, the inn has 8 rooms; book well in advance.

The Seafood Restaurant ££–£££ *Bruce Embankment, St Andrews tel: 01334-479475, www.theseafoodrestaurant. com.* Open daily for lunch and dinner. Where better to eat seafood than in this classy restaurant with a beautiful view over the water. Serves up lobster, prawns, scallops and much more.

The Silver Darling £££ *Pocra Quay, Aberdeen, tel: 01224-576229, www.thesilverdarling.co.uk.* Open Monday–Friday for lunch, Monday–Saturday for dinner. Superb seafood which varies depending on the daily catch. 'Silver Darling' is the local nickname for herring.

HIGHLANDS AND ISLANDS

Badachro Inn ££ *By Gairloch, tel: 01445-741255, www. badachroinn.com.* Open daily for lunch and dinner. Delightful setting overlooking Loch Gairloch for this popular pub with a plesant garden. The daily changing menus highlight locally caught seafood and there is a wide choice of real ale, wine or malt whisky.

Café 1 ££ *75 Castle Street, Inverness, tel: 01463-226200, www.cafe1.net.* Open Monday–Saturday for lunch and dinner. Located in the town centre, this well-reputed restaurant offers new Scottish cuisine. Reservations recommended.

Chandlery Restaurant ££ *In the Bosville Hotel, Portree, Skye, tel: 01478-612846, www.bosvillehotel.co.uk.* Open daily for lunch and dinner. The cuisine is outstanding: fresh seafood is a speciality, as are Aberdeen Angus beef and venison. The dishes are seasoned with locally grown herbs and accompanied by local organic vegetables. Reservations are a must.

The Three Chimneys £££–££££ *Colbost (near Dunvegan), Skye, tel: 01470-511258, www.threechimneys.co.uk.* Open Monday–Saturday lunch, daily dinner. Check opening times in winter. This is an award-winning restaurant that offers fine food using local ingredients in charming surroundings. Rooms are also available if you want to stay overnight.

The Water's Edge Restaurant £££ *Tobermory Hotel, Main Street, Tobermory, Isle of Mull, tel: 01688-302091, www. thetobermoryhotel.com.* Open daily for dinner only. The menu is full of local specialities such as Lagganulva lamb and Croig lobster and crab, and there's a good selection of Scottish cheeses. Children are welcome.

A–Z TRAVEL TIPS

A Summary of Practical Information

A

ACCOMMODATION (see also CAMPING, YOUTH HOSTELS AND REC-
OMMENDED HOTELS)

There is a great variety of accommodation in Scotland: hotels, guest
houses, manor houses, castles and bed-and-breakfasts. The Scottish
Tourist Board inspects and grades many of these establishments.
There are also hundreds of self-catering cottages, caravans, chalets
and crofts (small farmhouses). Farmhouse holidays and accommodation in private homes are other possibilities. The tourist office
can supply information about all these options.

Hotels vary greatly in standards. Many of the most pleasant are
converted country mansions in isolated settings. Some hotels have
swimming pools, and about 20 have their own golf courses.

Book ahead for Easter, and July–September. Most tourist offices
offer 'local bed-booking' services which assure overnight accommodation on the same day. You pay a minimal deposit for the reser-
vation, which is deducted from your bill. Some tourist boards also
charge a small booking fee.

VisitScotland *(for contact details see page 131)* lists hotels that
have special facilities for disabled visitors and young children, and
those that offer low-season prices for senior citizens.

Guest houses and bed-and-breakfast (B&B) premises can be great
bargains, though you'll sometimes have to share a bathroom. Most
establishments have a restaurant or can arrange for an evening meal.

AIRPORTS

Scotland has four major airports – Glasgow, Edinburgh, Prestwick
and Aberdeen – and some 25 minor airfields scattered about on the
mainland and the islands that are served by Loganair.

Glasgow Airport handles much of Scotland's air traffic. It is a 9-
mile (15-km), 20-minute taxi or bus ride from the city centre. Buses,
including the Glasgow Flyer, travel every 10–30 minutes between the

airport and Buchanan bus station in central Glasgow. Buses from the Buchanan station travel to Edinburgh (about 45 minutes) and other destinations in Scotland.

Edinburgh Airport handles UK, European and a couple of transatlantic services, but is beginning to rival Glasgow in receiving international flights. The airport is 7 miles (11km) from Edinburgh, and is linked with Waverley railway station at Waverley Bridge, in the city centre by a special airlink bus service that leaves every 10 minutes and takes about 30 minutes. Taxis are available just outside the arrival hall.

Prestwick Airport, about one hour from Glasgow (32 miles/ 51km), handles European and domestic flights. The modern terminal has its own train station, with services to Glasgow every half-hour. Public buses run to Glasgow and destinations in Ayrshire.

Aberdeen Airport, a 7-mile (11-km), 35-minute bus ride from Aberdeen station, serves mainly British and European destinations.

B

BICYCLE HIRE

Scotland offers many cycling opportunities. Local firms at tourist resorts will rent bicycles by the hour, day, or week. The Scottish Tourist Board issues a free pamphlet listing many rental firms. Book ahead for July or August. *See page 90* for information about biking trails.

BUDGETING FOR YOUR TRIP

Although good value for money is still the general rule in Scotland, bargains are rare and inflation relentlessly does its familiar work.

Accommodation: Double in moderately priced hotel with breakfast, £50–60 per person. Double per person in guest house with breakfast £30–40. Bed-and-breakfast (without bath), £25–30 per person.

Airport transfer: Edinburgh: bus £3.50 (£6 return), taxi about £20. Glasgow: bus (Glasgow Flyer) £4.50 (£6.50 return), taxi £18; Citylink bus between Edinburgh city centre and Glasgow Airport (standard ticket) £11.50 (£17.30 return).

Bicycle hire: £10–15 per day, £50–70 per week.

Buses: Edinburgh–Glasgow (standard tickets) £6.30 (£9.40 return). Explorer Pass: 3 days £35; 16 days (8 days of travel) £79; www.citylink.co.uk. City and local buses: fares depend on distance. Minimum bus fare in Edinburgh is £1.20 and £3 for 3 or more journeys in a day. Glasgow bus fares start at £1.02; exact fare is required.

Campsites: £8–12 per tent per night.

Meals: Lunch in pub or café £6–10; moderately priced restaurant meal with wine £18–25; afternoon tea £7; a pint of beer ranges from £2.50–3.20.

Shopping: Pure wool tartan, about £40 per metre; cashmere scarf, from around £25; kilt: man's £280, woman's £150–200; cashmere sweater from £100; lambswool sweater £25–40.

Sights: Most museums are free. Castles and gardens, £2–10.

Taxis: Basic rate (Edinburgh) begins at £1.60; increases by 25p every 210m/yds until 11.30pm, then for every 242m/yds; £1.10p extra after 6pm.

Tours: City on-and-off bus tours £12; sightseeing day tours £12–20; cruises from one hour to full day £10–40.

Trains: Prices vary according to day or time of travel. Glasgow–Edinburgh £10.60 off-peak travel one way. Freedom of Scotland pass (accepted on trains, buses and most ferries): 8 days (4 days of travel) £114, 15 days (8 days of travel) £153. Saver one-way fares (on First ScotRail services only and bought at least one day in advance): London–Edinburgh £44.50; Edinburgh–Inverness £10.30; Glasgow–Aberdeen £10.30; www.thetrainline.com.

C

CAMPING

There are more than 600 campsites in Scotland. The most elaborate have hot showers, flush toilets, laundry facilities and shops and can offer nature trails, forest walks and even access to golf courses. Many sites are more basic, with just a handful of pitches. To camp or caravan on private land you must have the owner's permission.

See VisitScotland's website www.visitscotland.com for more information. Some of the most attractive locations are operated by the Forestry Commission; visit www.forestry.gov.uk/scotland or write to: Information Branch, Forestry Commission, 231 Corstorphine Road, Edinburgh EH12 7 AT for its listings.

CAR HIRE

As a rule, it is cheaper to book a hire car before you leave on your trip. Be sure to check whether your credit card covers insurance. A medium-sized compact family car £230 per week, £55 per day, including VAT, unlimited mileage, but not insurance. Prices vary widely according to season. Beware hidden extras.

To hire a car you must be 21 or more years of age and have held a driver's licence for at least 12 months. Valid drivers' licences from almost all countries are recognised by the British authorities.

Major car rental companies are: Avis, tel: 0844-581 0147, www. avis.co.uk; Budget, tel: 0870-153 9170, www.budget.co.uk; Europcar, tel: 0870-607 5000, www.2.europcar.co.uk; Hertz, tel: 0870-844 8844, www.hertz.com. For competitive rates, try Arnold Clark, tel: 0141-237 4374, www. arnoldclarkrental.co.uk.

CLIMATE

The best months to visit Scotland are May and June, which have the most hours of sunshine and comparatively little rain. There aren't many of the midges and other stinging insects that become a problem, especially on the west coast, in full summer.

CLOTHING

Even if you're holidaying in Scotland in midsummer, take warm clothing and rainwear. Anoraks are very useful: buy a bright colour to make yourself conspicuous to hunters if you're going to be hiking or climbing. Sturdy shoes are a must both for outdoor walking and traversing cobblestone streets.

Scotland makes some of the world's best clothing, and you'll find a fine selection of knits, woollens and tweeds, although not at significantly lower prices than elsewhere in the UK.

CRIME AND SAFETY

As everywhere, crime in Scotland can be a problem, but even Glasgow, with Scotland's highest crime rate, is not dangerous by world standards. Take all the usual precautions. Honesty, however, is still quite prevalent in Scotland, even in the cities.

D

DRIVING

Road Conditions. A limited number of motorways connect Glasgow and Edinburgh with other major cities and areas. Be aware that most A roads are winding, two-lane roads, often skirting Scotland's many lochs and they can be slow-going. A surprise to most visitors are the single-lane roads found in the hinterland and on the islands. Most of these are paved, with passing places for giving way to oncoming traffic or allowing cars behind you to overtake (thank the driver who pulls over for you). Obviously, you should never park in these essential passing places. The twisting roads, along with the need for pulling in and out of the side slips, will more than double your normal driving time even over short distances. Other obstacles include sheep and cattle that often wander onto minor roads. Signposting is adequate, but a good map is essential.

Rules and regulations. The same basic rules apply in all of Britain. Drive on the left, overtake on the right. Turn left on a roundabout (traffic circle); at a junction where no road has priority, yield to traffic coming from the right. Seat belts must be worn. Drinking and driving is regarded as a serious offence and penalties are severe, involving loss of licence, heavy fines, and even prison sentences, and the law is strictly enforced.

To bring a car into Scotland you'll need registration and insurance papers and a driver's licence. Overseas visitors driving their own cars will need Green Card insurance as well.

Speed limits. In built-up areas, 30 or 40mph (48 or 65km/h); on major roads, 60mph (96km/h); on dual carriageways and motorways, 70mph (112km/h).

Fuel. Petrol is sold by the Imperial gallon (about 20 percent more voluminous than the US gallon) and by the litre; pumps show both measures. Four-star grade is 97 octane and three-star is 94 octane. Unleaded petrol is widely available. Most petrol stations are self-service. In the more remote areas stations are rather scarce, so take advantage when you see one.

If you need help. Members of automobile clubs that are affiliated with the British Automobile Association (AA) or the Royal Automobile Club (RAC) can benefit from speedy, efficient assistance in the event of a breakdown. If this should happen to you, AA members should tel: 0800-887 766, RAC members tel: 0800-828 282. Green Flag Motoring Assistance, tel: 0800-051 0636, (free to members or you may join on the spot).

Parking. There are meters in major centres and vigilant corps of traffic police and wardens to ticket violators, even in small towns. Ticket machines take most coins and some now take credit cards. Do not park on double yellow lines.

In Edinburgh and Glasgow, your car is best left in a car park. Buchanan Galleries, opposite Buchanan bus station in Glasgow, has a large multistorey car park (enter from Cathedral/Bath Street or Killermont Street). In Edinburgh, Castle Terrace is a large multistorey car park near Edinburgh Castle; St James' Centre (enter on York Place) is at the east end of Princes Street.

Road signs. Many standard international picture signs are displayed in Scotland. Distances are shown in miles. In the Highlands and islands only, road signs may appear first in Gaelic, then English.

E

ELECTRICITY

Throughout Scotland it's 230 volts AC, 50 Hz. Certain appliances may need a converter. Americans will need an adapter.

EMBASSIES AND CONSULATES

Many countries have consuls or other representatives in Edinburgh, but others only have representation in London.

Australia: Australian Consulate, Capital House, 2 Festival Square, EH3 9SU, tel: 0131-228 4771

Canada: Canadian Consulate, Burness, 50 Lothian Road, Edinburgh EG3 9WJ, tel: 0131-473 6320.

US: American Consulate General, 3 Regent Terrace, Edinburgh EH7 5BN; tel: 0131-556 8315.

EMERGENCIES

To call the fire brigade, police, ambulance, coast guard, lifeboat, or mountain rescue service, dial 999 from any telephone. You need no coin. Tell the emergency operator which service you need.

G

GAY AND LESBIAN TRAVELLERS

Scotland is a conservative country and the gay scene is found primarily in Edinburgh and Glasgow; both have lively gay pubs and nightclubs. The centre of Edinburgh's gay community is Broughton Street at the east end of town. The Edinburgh Gay and Lesbian Switchboard number is tel: 0131-556 4049; the Glasgow Gay and Lesbian Switchboard is tel: 0141-847 0447.

GETTING THERE

By air.

From North America. Direct transatlantic flights to Glasgow from Toronto are offered by Canadian Affair and Air Transat (Toronto, Calgary, Vancouver), US Airways (Philadelphia and Orlando), Continental Airlines (Newark, NJ). Flights from a variety of US hubs route flights via London or Amsterdam.

From Australia and New Zealand. Qantas and British Airways offer nonstop flights from Sydney and Melbourne to London. Air New Zealand has daily flights to London from Auckland.

From England and Republic of Ireland. There are direct services from all parts of the UK on British Airways, bmi, flybe, EasyJet and Ryanair, including frequent departures from Birmingham, Heathrow, Gatwick, Stansted, Southampton, Bristol and Manchester. Aer Lingus and Ryanair have regular flights from Dublin.

From Europe. Air France, bmi, KLM, Spanair, Lufthansa, Ryanair and EasyJet have direct flights from continental Europe to either Glasgow, Edinburgh or Aberdeen.

Air fares. The highest air fare are from June to September; fares in other months of the year may be considerably lower. All airlines offer economy fares: PEX, APEX, etc. These are subject to restrictions – for example, APEX flights have to be booked at least 14 days in advance and tickets are not refundable.

From the US, a direct flight to London with a domestic flight to Glasgow may be the cheapest option. Many American airlines offer a variety of package deals, both for group travel and for those who wish to travel independently. Packages include airfare, accommodation and travel between holiday destinations and may include some meals.

By rail. The train journey from London King's Cross to Edinburgh takes 4½ hours, and from London Euston to Glasgow takes 5½ hours. A sleeper service is available from London (Euston) to Glasgow, Edinburgh, Aberdeen, Inverness and Fort William. Economy fares are offered.

Visitors can take advantage of a variety of special fare plans that operate in Scotland. The **Freedom of Scotland Travelpass** is available for either 4 days of travel over 8 consecutive days, or 8 days of travel over 15 consecutive days. The pass gives unlimited travel on many bus routes and Caledonian MacBrayne ferries as well as on Scotland's rail network. It can be purchased at ScotRail stations and selected English travel centres. Travelpass holders can obtain a 20 percent reduction on NorthLink sailings from Aberdeen or Stromness to Orkney and Shetland. You can also choose from a selection of Rail Rover tickets; enquire at railway stations.

Visitors from abroad who wish to tour by rail can buy a **BritRail Pass** www.britrail.com before leaving their home countries, available from agents such as Rail Europe www.raileurope.com. These offer unlimited travel on the railway network throughout Scotland, England and Wales during a consecutive period of 4, 8, 15, 22 days, or a month. The **Flexipass** allows journeys to be made on nonconsecutive days; for example, 4 days unlimited travel over an 8-day period. Children aged 5 to 15 pay half price. The **BritRail Youth Pass** is for youngsters aged 16–25. None of these can be purchased in Britain.

By road. From London the quickest route is to take the M1 north to connect with the A1. If you are in the west, the M5 merges with the M6 and connects with the M74 to Glasgow.

To take your own car to Scotland, you will need proof of ownership and insurance documents, including Green Card insurance.

There are frequent coach services from all over Britain to various Scottish destinations by **National Express** and **Scottish Citylink**.

By sea. Ferry services from Northern Ireland operate from Larne to Troon and Belfast to Stranraer.

GUIDES AND TOURS

Dozens of bus tours are available in Scotland. Scotline Tours and Timberbush Tours, based in Edinburgh, offer two-day, full-day and half-day tours to St Andrews, Loch Lomond, Loch Ness, the Borders and other destinations; Gray Line and Glasgow-based Scottish Tours offer similar options. All tours can be booked through the tourist information offices, at Princes Mall in Edinburgh and George Square in Glasgow. Tour operators, centres, and hotels provide package holidays for sports such as golf and other outdoor sports.

Both Glasgow and Edinburgh have a number of city hop-on-hop-off bus tours. Tours originate at George Square in Glasgow and along Waverley Bridge in Edinburgh. Edinburgh Bus Tours and LRT Classic Tours in Edinburgh.

Details of guides and tours can also be had from The Secretary, Scottish Tour Guides Association, Norrie's House, 18b Broad Street, Stirling, FK8 1EF, tel: 01786-447784; www.stga.co.uk. Members of this association wear official badges engraved with their names. Most are based in Edinburgh, Glasgow, Aberdeen and Dundee. Some will accompany tours.

H

HEALTH AND MEDICAL CARE

Scotland, home of much pioneering work in medicine, is proud of the high standard of its health care. Medical care is free for EU (on production of the EHIC card) and Commonwealth residents under the National Health Service (NHS). Other nationals should check to be sure they have adequate health insurance coverage. US residents should be aware that Medicare does not apply outside the United States.

Emergency care. Major hospitals with 24-hour emergency service are: Edinburgh Royal Infirmary, tel: 0131-536 1000; Glasgow Royal Infirmary, tel: 0141-211 4000; Aberdeen Royal Infirmary, tel: 0845-456 6000; and Inverness Raigmore tel: 01463-704000.

Pharmacies. In Edinburgh, Glasgow and a few other major centres you should find a duty chemist (drugstore) open until 9pm; otherwise, contact a police station for help in filling in an emergency prescription, or dial 999.

Tourist Information Offices can advise you on the duty chemist in your area.

Insects. In the summer midges are a nuisance or worse, especially on Scotland's west coast. Clegs (horse flies) and tiny but devilish berry bugs also attack in warmer weather. Insect repellents aren't always effective; ask the advice of a chemist.

L

LANGUAGE

Gaelic and old Scottish words and phrases in everyday use will baffle the most fluent English speaker. Today just over 60,000 Scots speak Gaelic, most of them residents of the Western Isles. English spoken with a strong Scots accent can take a while to get used to and place names are often not pronounced the way you'd expect: Kirkcudbright is Kir*coo*bree, Culzean is Cul*lane*, Colquhoun is Co-*hoon*, Culross is *Coorus*, Menzies is *Mingies*, Dalziell is *Dee*-ell. Here are some examples to help you along:

Scottish/Gaelic	English
aber	river mouth
Auld Reekie	Edinburgh (Old Smoky)
ben	mountain
bide a wee	wait a bit
biggin	building
brae	hillside
bramble	blackberry
brig	bridge

burn	stream
cairn	pile of stones as landmark
ceilidh	song/story gathering
clachan	hamlet
croft	small land-holding
dinna fash yersel'	don't get upset
eilean	island
fell	hill
firth	estuary
gait	street
ghillie	attendant to hunting or fishing
glen	valley
haud yer wheesht	shut up
inver	mouth of river
ken	know
kirk	church
kyle	strait, narrows
lang may yer lum reek	long may your chimney smoke (i.e. may you have a long life)
link	dune
linn	waterfall
loch	lake
mickle	small amount
mull	promontory
ness	headland
provost	mayor
sett	tartan pattern
skirl	shriek of bagpipes
strath	river valley
thunderplump	thunderstorm
tolbooth	old courthouse/jail
wynd	lane, alley

M

MAPS

Free maps and helpful directions are available at any tourism office. For driving, a good map is essential. Collins's *Touring Map of Scotland* is published in association with VisitScotland. Collins also publishes street atlases of Edinburgh and Glasgow and the *A–Z Street Atlas* is available for both cities. Route maps for hiking and biking are available from the tourist office; you may also want to buy one of the series of ordinance maps that are available.

MEDIA

Television: Viewers in Scotland have plenty of choice with two main BBC channels and several commercial channels. Digital television services provide a wide range of extra channels. Many larger hotels offer a variety of cable and satellite TV channels and pay-per-view films.
Radio: Radio Scotland is the main BBC radio service and national BBC radio stations also operate in Scotland. A range of commercial radio stations cater for different areas of Scotland. Various international stations can also be received.
Newspapers and magazines: In addition to British national newspapers, Scottish daily papers are: the *Herald* (published in Glasgow), the *Scotsman* (published in Edinburgh), the *Daily Record*, and the *Aberdeen Press and Journal.* Details of events and entertainment in and around Glasgow and Edinburgh are given in the magazine *The List,* published every two weeks. The *International Herald Tribune,* edited in Paris, and US weekly news magazines are sold in the major centres and at airports.

MONEY

Currency. The pound sterling (£) is a decimal monetary unit and is divided into 100 pence (p). Coins consist of 1p, 2p, 5p, 10p, 20p, 50p, £1 and £2; and banknotes consist of £1 (a few Scottish notes are still in circulation), £5, £10, £20, £50, and £100.

Scottish banks issue their own notes, which are not, technically, legal tender in England and Wales, although many shops will accept them and English banks will readily change them for you.

Currency exchange. You will get the best exchange rate for your foreign currency at banks (see Opening Hours); currency exchange bureaux rarely offer as good a rate, and you'll get the worst rate at your hotel. Many Tourist Information Offices have currency exchange facilities.

Credit cards. Major credit cards can be used in most hotels, restaurants, petrol stations and shops – signs are usually displayed indicating which are accepted.

Travellers' cheques. Travellers' cheques are accepted throughout Scotland. You'll need your passport when cashing them, and banks will charge a fee. The American Express office will cash its own travellers' cheques without a fee.

OPENING HOURS

Opening hours may vary from place to place. However, **banks** are usually open Monday–Friday 9am–5pm, with branches in city centres open on Saturday mornings. Banks in small towns may close for lunch. Some rural areas are served only by mobile banks that arrive at regular intervals and stay for a few hours.

Offices and businesses are usually open Monday–Friday 9am–5pm; some have Saturday hours.

Post offices are open Monday–Friday 9am–5.30pm and Saturday 9am–12.30pm. Sub-stations have a half-day closing on Wednesday or Thursday.

Shop hours are normally Monday–Saturday 9am–5.30pm, some until 7pm or 8pm on Thursday. Most shops in villages and smaller towns close on Sunday and may close for lunch. In the larger cities in major shopping areas, shops open at either 11am or noon on Sunday and close at 5pm or 5.30pm.

Museums and sightseeing attractions have greatly varying opening hours. As a rule, attractions are open from about 9.30am until late afternoon, or early evening in summer. In winter many castles and other places of interest are closed to the public or open for limited periods. It's best to call for information. Museums in the cities are generally open Monday–Saturday 10am–5pm and noon–5pm on Sunday.

Major **tourist information offices** are open all year round, usually Monday–Saturday 9am–8pm and Sunday 10am–8pm in July and August. At other times of the year, they close earlier.

P

POLICE

Scottish police do not carry guns. Police patrol cars usually have yellow stripes and a blue light.

The emergency telephone number for police aid is **999** all over the country. You can also dial 0 and ask for the police.

POST OFFICES

Letters and packages sent within the UK can use the first- or second-class postal service. Because second-class mail may be slow, it's advisable to pay the modest extra postage for first class. Postcards and letters to Europe and elsewhere overseas automatically go by airmail. The post office offers an express mail service, Parcelforce International.

Stamps are sold at post offices (found in almost every Scottish village even if they share space with grocery shops) and newsagents, as well as from vending machines. Postboxes are red and come in many shapes and sizes.

Edinburgh's main post office is at 8–10 St James' Centre. For postal information, tel: 0845-722 3344. Glasgow's main post office is 47 St Vincent Street, tel: 0845-722 3344.

Postage: within the UK 36p; to Europe and the rest of world, air-mail 60p.

PUBLIC HOLIDAYS

Bank holidays in Scotland are not always closing days for offices and shops. Many towns have their individual holidays, generally on a Monday. VisitScotland publishes an annual list of local and national holidays and the chart below is a guide to fixed holidays. If one falls on a Saturday or Sunday, it is usual to take off the following Monday.

1 January	New Year's Day
2 January	Bank Holiday
25 December	Christmas Day
26 December	Boxing Day
Moveable dates:	
March or April	Good Friday/Easter Monday
May	Spring Bank Holiday
August	Summer Bank Holiday

1 January	New Year's Day
2 January	Bank Holiday
25 December	Christmas Day
26 December	Boxing Day
Moveable dates:	
March or April	Good Friday/Easter Monday
May	Spring Bank Holiday
August	Summer Bank Holiday

T

TELEPHONES

Public phones are located in pubs, restaurants, post offices, shops and in the street. BT booths can usually accept coins, phonecards or credit/debit cards. Internet kiosks are also available. Many phones in small towns and public buildings are still coin-operated, usually accepting 10p (minimum fee is 60p), 20p, 50p and £1 coins. Some boxes take euro coins.

Public phone booths display information on overseas dialling codes and the international exchange. Dial 118 505 for international directory inquiries, 155 for an international operator. For local directory inquiries, dial 118 500, and for operator assistance, dial 100. To make a local reverse-charge call, dial 100 and ask the operator to reverse the charges. Talking Pages will give you a specific number for any kind of place or service you may be looking for in any area.

Mobile (cell) phone coverage is not as good in Scotland as the rest of the UK as only around 92 per cent of the country is covered, with rural areas particularly neglected by service providers. Coverage varies extensively between different mobile phone companies. You will need a GSM cellular phone for use in Scotland. It is possible to rent these but this is an expensive option, especially for a short stay. If you have a GSM phone the roaming charges may well be high. The cheapest option is to buy a local UK SIM card to use in the GSM phone; incoming calls will be free and local calls inexpensive. Check out all the options before travelling.

TIME ZONES

Scotland, like the rest of the United Kingdom, is on Greenwich Mean Time. Between April and October clocks are put forward one hour.

New York	**Edinburgh**	Jo'burg	Sydney	Auckland
7am	**noon**	1pm	9pm	11pm

TIPPING

While tipping is customary in Scotland, there's no pressure. Hotels and restaurants may add a service charge to your bill, in which case tipping is not really necessary. If service is not included, add about 10 percent to your bill. Many cafés and informal restaurants have a box for tips beside the cash register.

Tip hotel porters about £1 per bag, and tip your hotel maid about £5 per week. Lavatory attendants should get 20–50p. Your taxi driver will be pleased with 10 percent, and so will your tour guide. Hairdressers should get 10–20 percent.

TOURIST INFORMATION

There is probably no tourist destination in the world that produces more information for visitors than Scotland. Strategically placed throughout the Lowlands, Highlands and Islands are some 150 tourist information centres, offering a wide range of publications, free or for sale, as well as expert advice. For a complete list of their addresses, write to the headquarters of VisitScotland (formerly the Scottish Tourist Board) at the address below. They're identified by blue-and-white signs with an italicised *i* (for 'information').

In Edinburgh the **Tourist Information Centre** is in Princes Street Mall, 3 Princes Street, tel: 0845-225 5121, or there's an Information and Accommodation Service at Edinburgh Airport. In Glasgow, the information centre is at 11 George Square; tel: 0141-204 4400.

The national headquarters of **VisitScotland** (www.visitscotland. com) is at Ocean Point One, 94 Ocean Drive, Edinburgh; tel: 0131-472-2222. Don't turn up here for help; only written and telephone inquiries are accepted. National tourist information can be supplied by any major tourist information centre in Scotland. For further information on Scotland and the rest of Britain check www.visitbritain.com. In London you can drop into the Britain and London Visitor Centre, 1 Regent Street, London SW1Y 4XT; tel: 0870-156 6366.

TRANSPORT

Scotland's extensive public transport network can be of considerable use to tourists. If you're touring the north without a car, a Travelpass *(see page 122)* enables you to travel on most coaches, trains and ferries operating in the Highlands and Islands at a significant saving. Maps, timetables and brochures are available free from tourist offices and transport terminals *(see pages 131)*. There are also money-saving excursions, weekend and island-to-island ferry schemes. On the Western Isles post buses are scheduled to link up with ferry services.

City transport. Most Scottish towns and cities have good bus services, particularly Edinburgh and Glasgow. Night bus services in cities are less frequent. Family and other discount tickets are available in Edinburgh at the Lothian Buses Travelshop at Waverley Bridge, tel: 0131-555 6363. The First Bus company serves urban and rural areas around Edinburgh. In Glasgow, the main bus company is First Bus; contact the Travel Centre at St Enoch Square, tel: 0141-226 4826.

Glasgow also has a simple but efficient subway system, nicknamed 'the Clockwork Orange', which operates in the city centre. Trains are frequent and the standard charge is £1.20. The Park and Ride scheme involves parking your car at certain underground stations on the outskirts of the city and then taking the subway into the centre.

Coaches. Comfortable and rapid long-distance coaches with toilets link the major towns. For details, call **National Express**, tel: 0871-781 8181; **Scottish Citylink**, tel: 0871-266 3333; or **Buchanan Street Bus Station**, tel: 0141-333 3708. Citylink offers the Explorer Pass for three days' travel out of five, five days' travel out of ten or eight days out of 16, good on both major and local routes.

Trains. Train services include the Inter-City trains, with principal routes from London to Glasgow's Central Station (5½ hours) and to Edinburgh's Waverley Station (4½ hours); there are day and night trains. From Glasgow's Queen Street Station, routes continue on to Perth, Dundee, Aberdeen and Inverness and there are smaller, secondary lines. For **National Rail Enquiries**, tel: 0845-748 4950; www.nationalrail.co.uk.

Ferries. Ferries to the Western Isles are generally run by **Caledonian MacBrayne**, tel: 01475-650100; NorthLink Ferries, tel: 0845-

600 0449, connect with Orkney and Shetland. There are ferry services from Aberdeen to Lerwick and from Scrabster to Stromness. There are also many ferries between the islands. Reservations are essential in peak season for the more popular car ferries.

Taxis. In Scotland's major centres you'll find most taxis are black, London-style cabs. A taxi's yellow 'For Hire' sign is lit when it's available for hire. There are taxi ranks at airports and stations, and you can hail them on the street. Major centres have 24-hour radio taxi services. There's an extra charge for luggage. If you hire a taxi for a long-distance trip, negotiate the price with the driver before setting off.

TRAVELLERS WITH DISABILITIES

Capability Scotland is Scotland's leading disability organisation, providing a range of flexible services which support disabled people of all ages in their everyday lives. Contact: Capability Scotland, 11 Ellersly Road, Edinburgh EH12 6HY; tel: 0131-337 9876, fax: 0131-346 7864, www.capability-scotland.org.uk.

V

VISAS AND ENTRY REQUIREMENTS

For non-British citizens the same formalities apply at Scottish ports of entry as elsewhere in the UK. Citizens of EU countries need only an identity card. Visitors from the US and most Commonwealth countries need only a valid passport for stays of up to 6 months.

On arrival at a British port or airport, if you have goods to declare you follow the red channel; with nothing to declare you take the green route, bypassing inspection, although customs officers may make random spot checks. Free exchange of non-duty-free goods for personal use is permitted between EU countries and the UK. Duty-free items are still subject to restrictions: check before you go. There's no limit on the amount of currency you can bring into or take out of Britain.

W

WEBSITES AND INTERNET ACCESS

The following are some useful websites for planning your visit.
Tourism:

www.visitbritain.com British Tourist Authority

www.edinburgh.org Edinburgh and Lothians

www.seeglasgow.com Greater Glasgow and Clyde Valley

www.undiscoveredscotland.co.uk Undiscovered Scotland

www.scotland.org.uk Travel Scotland

www.visitscotland.com Visit Scotland

General:

www.historic-scotland.gov.uk Historic Scotland

www.nts.org.uk National Trust for Scotland

www.scotsman.com The *Scotsman*

Scotland is well serviced when it comes to internet access, with even
some of the remotest locations supported by dial-up, broadband or
even Wi-Fi. Larger towns and cities in Scotland have internet cafés
and you will increasingly find hotels and guest houses offer internet and wireless access; many B & Bs are yet to follow suit. Public
libraries across Scotland offer free (limited time) internet access providing that you register on arrival.

Y

YOUTH HOSTELS

The **Scottish Youth Hostels Association** runs around 70 hostels.
Visitors can stay without being members of the association but
membership brings many benefits, including reduced prices for
rooms. Their address is 7 Glebe Crescent, Stirling FK8 2JA; tel:
01786-891 400 or 0845-293 77373 for reservations, www.
syha.org.uk. Hostels are graded by the VisitScotland quality as-
surance scheme.

Recommended Hotels

Accommodation around Scotland covers a wide spectrum, from the basic B&B (bed-and-breakfast) to modern luxury hotels and ancient refurbished castles. VisitScotland (*see page 131*) publishes many brochures and booklets detailing available accommodation, prices, facilities, etc.

Below you will find a selection of accommodation chosen for its quality and value for money. Prices are based on two people sharing a double room with breakfast in high season. Keep in mind that prices vary according to time of year and availability. All rooms have bath or shower and all establishments take major credit cards unless otherwise indicated. Edinburgh is extremely busy during the Edinburgh Festival (August), so book well in advance if you plan to visit the capital during that period.

££££ over £200	**££** £80–£140
£££ £140–£200	**£** below £80

EDINBURGH

Albyn Townhouse £–££ *16 Hartington Gardens, EH10 4LD, tel: 0131-229 6459, www.albyntownhouse.co.uk.* Striking four-storey 19th-century Victorian townhouse in a peaceful cul-de-sac, yet within walking distance or short bus ride of the Old Town. Good breakfast and attentive service. 10 rooms.

The Balmoral ££££ *1 Princes St, EH2 2EQ, tel: 0131-556 2414, www.thebalmoralhotel.com.* This grand hotel has long been a legend. In a commanding position at the east end of Princes Street, it has a distinguished décor, large bedrooms and one of Edinburgh's best restaurants. 188 rooms.

Bank Hotel ££ *1 South Bridge St, EH1 1LL, tel: 0131-556 9940, www.festival-inns.co.uk.* Conveniently located on the Royal Mile, this quirky hotel in a former bank building has comfortable, well-kept rooms, each a homage to a famous Scot, above a rather splendid café-bar serving good pub-style food. 9 rooms.

Caledonian Hilton Hotel ££££ *Princes Street, EH1 2AB, tel: 0131-222 8888, www.hilton.co.uk/caledonian.* One of the city's landmarks, this traditional luxury hotel is at the western end of bustling Princes Street, with views of Edinburgh Castle. Modern Scottish cuisine. Some rooms are adapted for disabled visitors. 249 rooms.

Channings Hotel ££–£££ *12–16 South Learmouth Gardens, EH4 1EZ, tel: 0131-315 2226, www.townhousecompany.com/channings.* This hotel, in a tranquil residential setting, suggests a Scottish country house. It has a notable restaurant, and is about five minutes by bus or car from the city centre. Also bar serving meals, and a sundeck garden. 41 rooms.

The Glasshouse Hotel £££–££££ *2 Greenside Place, EH1 3AA, tel: 525 8200, www.theetoncollection.com.* Situated near the east end of Princes Street, this is a state-of-the-art building where the rooms surround a 2-acre roof garden. The exterior rooms have splendid views to the New Town or across the Firth of Forth. Breakfast is available on request, but the hotel has no restaurants: though there are many just minutes away. 65 rooms.

Hotel Missoni ££££ *1 George Bridge, EH1 1AD, tel: 0131-220 6666, www.hotelmissoni.com.* Perfectly placed on Edinburgh's Royal Mile, this splendid luxurious boutique hotel certainly has the wow factor. Fabulous design and stunning use of textiles. 136 rooms.

SOUTHEAST AND THE BORDERS

Burts Hotel ££ *Market Square, Melrose, TD6 9PN, tel: 01896-822 285, www.burtshotel.co.uk.* This family-run hotel is housed in a restored 1722 town house near the abbey. Rooms are airy and restful and the dining room serves good traditional Scottish food. Golf and fishing. 20 rooms.

Ednam House Hotel ££–£££ *Bridge Street, Kelso, TD5 7HT, tel: 01573-224168, www.ednamhouse.com.* This large hotel on the

River Tweed is housed in a mid-8th-century Georgian house; rooms have antiques and period furnishings. You can feast on good Scottish food while admiring the view of the river from the dining room. Golf and fishing, cycling paths and walks. 32 rooms. Closed Christmas season.

Greywalls Hotel ££££ *Duncur Road, Muirfield, Gullane, East Lothian, EH31 2EG, tel: 01620-842144, www.greywalls.co.uk.* This attractive Edwardian house was designed by noted architect Sir Edwin Lutyens, with gardens laid out by Gertrude Jekyll. With fine views and a good restaurant, it is a 40-minute drive from the centre of Edinburgh. Tennis and croquet; golf course nearby. Closed Jan–end April. 23 rooms.

Jedburgh Forest ££ *Jedburgh, TD8 6PJ, tel: 01835-840222, www.jedforesthotel.com.* Located 7 miles (11km) north of the border on the A68, Jedburgh Forest prides itself on being the first hotel you will encounter in Scotland. It is set in 35 acres of grounds with private fishing available. Good food served in elegant surroundings. 12 luxury rooms.

Knockinaam Lodge ££££ *Portpatrick, Dumfries and Galloway, DG9 9AD, tel: 01776-810471, www.knockinaamlodge.com.* Chic hunting lodge style Victorian hotel set in beautiful parkland. Fine sea views, excellent cuisine, fishing, superb walking. 10 luxury rooms.

GLASGOW

Angus Guest House £ *970 Sauchiehall Street, G3 7TH, tel: 0141-357 5155, www.angushotelglasgow.co.uk.* Near Kelvingrove Park and the art galleries, this small, friendly hotel is a good budget option where the staff are very helpful. 18 rooms.

Carlton George £££ *44 West George Street, G2 1DH, tel: 0141-353 6373, www.carlton.nl/george.* A modern, luxurious, state-of-the-art hotel in the heart of Glasgow. The Windows rooftop restaurant offers excellent Scottish cooking and great views. 64 rooms.

Malmaison £££ *278 West George Street, G2 4LL, tel: 0141-572 1000, www.malmaison.com.* Modern and trendy with beautifully decorated rooms, this former Greek Orthodox church still manages to preserve its important historical character. Restaurant serving Mediterranean cuisine. 72 rooms.

One Devonshire Gardens £££ *1 Devonshire Gardens, G12 0UX, tel: 0141-339 2001, www.hotelduvin.com.* In a leafy district west of the centre, this luxury boutique hotel is now part of the Hotel du Vin group and offers beautifully decorated rooms and impeccable service. 49 rooms.

Saint Judes ££ *190 Bath Street, G2 4HG, tel: 0141-352 8800, www.saintjudes.com.* Fashionable small boutique hotel with oodles of style. Good restaurant, sophisticated cocktail bar and attentive service. Mama San Bar is one of Glasgow's most stylish and exclusive nightclubs. 6 rooms.

CENTRAL SCOTLAND

Apex City Quay Hotel and Spa ££ *1 West Victoria Dock Road, Dundee, DD1 3JP, tel: 01382-202404, www.apexhotels.co.uk.* Located in the heart of the new City Quay development and overlooking the River Tay, this striking hotel is stylish and contemporary. Good food, plus spa, sauna and treament rooms. 152 rooms.

The Caledonian ££ *10 Union Terrace, Aberdeen, AB10 1WE, tel: 0871-376 9003, www.thistlehotels.com.* Centrally located Victorian building with modern facilities and elegant public rooms; restaurant and café/wine bar. 77 rooms.

Dalmunzie House Hotel ££–£££ *Spittal o' Glenshee, Blairgowrie, PH10 7QG, tel: 01250-885224, www.dalmunzie.com.* A mountain laird's mansion with splendid views, situated 18 miles (29km) north of Blairgowrie on the A93. Good home-cooking as well as fishing, golf and tennis. Conveniently located for the ski slopes. 17 rooms.

Dunfallandy Country House ££ *Pitlochry, PH16 5NA, tel: 01796-474128, www.dunfallandy.co.uk.* Just 2 miles (3km) south of Pitlochry, this Georgian house overlooks the town and has stunning views of the Tummel Valley. Complimentary afternoon tea on arrival and a first-rate breakfast. 3 rooms.

The George Hotel £–££ *Main Street East, Inveraray PA32 8TT, tel: 01499-302111, www.thegeorgehotel.co.uk.* The George has been sensitively restored over the last few years, with fine antiques and paintings a star feature. The pub part, with cocktail bar and conservatory restaurant, has stone floors and beamed ceilings. 17 rooms.

Kildrummy Castle Hotel £££ *Kildrummy by Alford, Aberdeenshire, AB33 8RA, tel: 01975-571288, www.kildrummycastlehotel. co.uk.* Victorian country house in baronial-castle style near the old castle ruins and Kildrummy Gardens. Fine dining. Closed January. 16 rooms.

Killiecrankie House Hotel ££ *Killiecrankie, By Pitlochry, Perthshire, tel: 01796-473220, www.killiecrankie hotel.co.uk.* This country-house hotel, in a scenic setting, is a good base for touring the area. Excellent meals. 10 rooms.

The Old Course Hotel ££££ *St Andrews, Fife KY16 9SP, tel: 01334-474371, www.oldcoursehotel.co.uk.* Modern luxury hotel adjoining historic golf course with good restaurants, indoor swimming pool, health spa and beauty salon. 102 rooms and 32 suites.

The Park Lodge Hotel ££ *32 Park Terrace, Stirling, FK8 2JS, tel: 01786-474862, www.parklodge.net.* An elegant hotel in a part-Victorian, part-Georgian mansion overlooking the castle and park. Rooms are furnished with antiques, some four-poster beds. 9 rooms.

Ramada Jarvis Perth ££ *West Mill Street, Perth, PH1 5QP, tel: 0844-815 9105, www.ramadajarvis.co.uk.* A comfortable hotel converted from a 15th-century water mill, set in charming gardens and ideally situated for Perth city centre. 76 rooms.

HIGHLANDS AND ISLANDS

The Arisaig Hotel £–££ *Arisaig, Inverness-shire, PH39 4NH, tel: 01687-450210, www.arisaighotel.co.uk.* Arisaig Hotel dates back to the Jacobite era, and was originally built as a coaching inn around 1720. The hotel looks across Arisaig Bay towards the Isles of Eigg and Muck. Varied menu. 13 rooms.

Bosville Hotel ££–£££ *Bosville Terrace, Portree, Skye, IV51 9DG, tel: 01478-612846, www.bosvillehotel.co.uk.* Stylish accommodation with views of Portree Harbour and Cuillin Hills; outstanding restaurant *(see page 112)*. 15 rooms.

Craigmonie Hotel ££ *9 Annfield Road, Inverness, IV2 3HX, tel: 01463-231649, www.swallow-hotels.com/craigmonie.* Situated in the heart of Inverness with the feel of a country dwelling, Craigmonie offers luxurious leisure activities and a delicious à la carte menu. 35 rooms.

Culloden House Hotel ££££ *Culloden, Inverness, IV1 7BZ, tel: 01463-790461, www.cullodenhouse.co.uk.* Georgian house close to the site of the 1746 battle, and 3 miles (5km) east of Inverness on the A96. Bonnie Prince Charlie slept here before the battle. Extensive gardens and parkland; facilities include tennis, sauna and solarium. Restaurant. 28 rooms.

Inverlochy Castle ££££ *Torlundy, Fort William, PH33 6SN, tel: 01397-702177, www.inverlochycastlehotel.com.* Luxury Victorian castle 3 miles (5km) northeast of Fort William on A82. Set in 50 acres (20 hectares) of woodland with splendid views of the loch and mountains. Fine cuisine, tennis, fishing. 17 rooms.

Kinloch Lodge £££ *Sleat, Skye, IV43 8QY, tel: 01471-833214, www.kinloch-lodge.co.uk.* This is the home of the chief of Clan Macdonald and his wife, who is a notable cook and cookbook author. The manor has been expanded from a 1680 hunting lodge and contains family portraits and possessions. The wonderful food is based on traditional Scottish cuisine made with local ingredients and the restaurant has been awarded a Michelin star. 15 rooms.

The Moorings Hotel ££ *Banavie, Fort William, PH33 7LY, tel: 01397-772797, www.moorings-fortwilliam.co.uk.* By the Caledonian Canal, the hotel has views of Ben Nevis. The pleasant bedrooms are nicely decorated. Award-winning restaurant. 27 rooms.

Scarista House £££ *Isle of Harris, Western Isles, HS3 3HX, tel: 01859-550238, www.scaristahouse.com.* This Georgian manse is set in a remote area overlooking a beach – perfect for getting away from it all. It has an outstanding restaurant. 5 rooms.

Summer Isles Hotel £££ *Achiltibuie, Ross-shire, IV26 2YG, tel: 01854-622282, www.summerisleshotel.co.uk.* Open Easter–October. Over the years the hotel has established itself as an oasis of civilisation hidden away in a stunningly beautiful, but still wild and untouched landscape. Nearly everything you eat here is home produced or locally caught. 10 rooms and 3 suites.

Tiroran House ££–£££ *Mull, PA69 6ES (off the road to Iona on B8035), tel: 01681-705232, www.tiroran.com.* This lovely country house is set in beautiful grounds with spacious lawns and gardens on the shore of Loch Scridain. Its public rooms and comfortable bedrooms are more like those in a home than a hotel. Good food is served in an elegant setting. Telephone for directions before you go or you'll run the risk of getting lost. 7 rooms plus cottages.

Western Isles Hotel ££ *Tobermory, Mull, PA75 6PR, tel: 01688-302012, www.westernisleshotel.co.uk* A welcoming atmosphere greets the visitor to this traditional hotel that has spectacular views over the Sound of Mull and Tobermory Bay. The food is excellent and served in the formal dining room or charming conservatory. 28 rooms.

INDEX

Berlitz pocket guide

Scotland

Fourth Edition 2011
Reprinted 2012

Written by Alice Fellows
Updated by Hilary Weston
Series Editor: Tom Stainer

Printed in China by CTPS

Berlitz Trademark Reg. U.S. Patent Office and other countries. Marca Registrada Used under licence from the Berlitz Investment Corporation

Photography credits
Alamy 57; APA Pete Bennett 3TR, 3MR, 15, 36, 94; Marcus Brooke 48, 78; APA David Cruickshanks, 1, 2TL, 3BR, 4BL, 6T, 6M, 6B, 7T, 7M, 8, 13, 26, 29, 31, 37, 38, 41, 43, 45, 52, 55, 59, 60, 63, 64, 67, 68, 71, 73, 75, 77, 79, 84, 86, 88, 90, 92, 95, 96, 98, 101, 102, 105; iStockphoto 21; Jerry Dennis 2BR, 10, 39, 49, 51, 93; Hulton/Getty 17; APA Douglas McGilveray 4-5, 4BM, 4TR, 5TL, 18, 24, 32; Jon Mountjoy 4TL; National Galleries of Scotland 20; Johnathan Smith 2BL, 2TR, 11, 28, 47, 62, 66, 74, 82, 83; Scottish Viewpoint 5BM, 5BR, 5TR; APA Bill Wassman 3ML, 3BL,, 44, 76, 80, 104
Cover picture: 4Corners Images

Contact us

At Berlitz we strive to keep our guides as accurate and up to date as possible, but if you find anything that has changed, or if you have any suggestions on ways to improve this guide, then we would be delighted to hear from you.

Berlitz Publishing, PO Box 7910, London SE1 1WE, England.
email: berlitz@apaguide.co.uk
www.berlitzpublishing.com